雙雙中文教材 (13)
Chinese Language and Culture Course

中國神話傳說 Chinese Myth and Legend

王雙雙 編著

圖書在版編目（CIP）數據

中國神話傳說：繁體版 / 王雙雙編著.—北京：北京大學出版社，2008.10
（雙雙中文教材·13）
ISBN 978-7-301-14205-9

I. 中… II. 王… III. 漢語–對外漢語教學–教材 IV. H195.4

中國版本圖書館CIP數據核字（2008）第134733號

書　　　　名：	中國神話傳說
著作責任者：	王雙雙 編著
英 文 翻 譯：	王亦兵
封 面 圖 案：	王金泰
責 任 編 輯：	孫　嫻
標 準 書 號：	ISBN 978-7-301-14205-9/H·2058
出 版 發 行：	北京大學出版社
地　　　　址：	北京市海淀區成府路205號　100871
網　　　　址：	http://www.pup.cn
電　　　　話：	郵購部 62752015　發行部 62750672　編輯部 62752028　出版部 62754962
電 子 信 箱：	zpup@pup.pku.edu.cn
印 刷 者：	北京大學印刷廠
經 銷 者：	新華書店
	889毫米×1194毫米　16開本　7.5印張　100千字
	2008年10月第1版　2008年10月第1次印刷
定　　　　價：	90.00元（含課本、練習冊和CD-ROM一張）

未經許可，不得以任何方式複製或抄襲本書之部分或全部內容。
版權所有，侵權必究
舉報電話：010-62752024
電子信箱：fd@pup.pku.edu.cn

前言

《雙雙中文教材》是一套專門為海外青少年編寫的中文課本,是我在美國八年的中文教學實踐基礎上編寫成的。在介紹這套教材之前,請讀一首小詩:

> 一雙神奇的手,
>
> 推開一扇窗。
>
> 一條神奇的路,
>
> 通向燦爛的中華文化。
>
> 鮑凱文 鮑維江
>
> 1998年

鮑維江和鮑凱文姐弟倆是美國生美國長的孩子,也是我的學生。1998年冬,他們送給我的新年賀卡上的小詩,深深地打動了我的心。我把這首詩看成我文化教學的回聲。我要傳達給海外每位中文老師:我教給他們(學生)中國文化,他們思考了、接受了、回應了。這條路走通了!

語言是交際的工具,更是一種文化和一種生活方式,所以學習中文也就離不開中華文化的學習。早期漢字的象形性較強,她從遠古走來,帶有大量的文化信息,但學起來並不容易。使學生增強興趣、減小難度,走出苦學漢字的怪圈,走進領悟中華文化的花園,是我編寫這套教材的初衷。

學生不論大小,天生都有求知的慾望,都有欣賞文化美的追求。中華文化本身是魅力十足的。把這宏大而玄妙的文化,深入淺出地,有聲有色地介紹出來,讓這迷人的文化如涓涓細流,一點一滴地滲入學生們的心田,使學生們逐步體味中國文化,是我編寫這套教材的目的。

為此我將漢字的學習放入文化介紹的流程之中同步進行,讓同學們在學中國地理的同時,學習漢字;在學中國歷史的同時,學習漢字;在學中國哲學的同時,學習漢字;在學中國科普文選的同時,學習漢字……

這樣的一種中文學習,知識性強,趣味性強;老師易教,學生易學。當學生們合上書本時,他們的眼前是中國的大好河山,是中國五千年的歷史和妙不可言的哲學思維,是奔騰的現代中國……

總之,他們瞭解中華文化,就會探索這片土地,熱愛這片土地,就會與中國結下情緣。

最後我要衷心地感謝所有熱情支持和幫助我編寫教材的老師、家長、學生、朋友和家人,特別是老同學唐玲教授、何茜老師、我姐姐王欣欣編審及我女兒Uta Guo年復一年的鼎力相助。可以說這套教材是大家努力的結果。

王雙雙

說　明

　　《雙雙中文教材》是一套專門為海外學生編寫的中文教材。它是由美國加州王雙雙老師和中國專家學者共同努力，在海外多年的實踐中編寫出來的。全書共20冊，識字量2500個，包括了從識字、拼音、句型、短文的學習，到初步的較系統的中國文化的學習。教材大體介紹了中國地理、歷史、哲學等方面的豐富內容，突出了中國文化的魅力。課本知識面廣，趣味性強，深入淺出，易教易學。

　　這套教材體系完整、構架靈活、使用面廣。學生可以從零起點開始，一直學完全部課程20冊；也可以將後11冊（10～20冊）的九個文化專題和第五冊（漢語拼音）單獨使用，這樣便於開設中國哲學、地理、歷史等專門課程以及假期班、短期中國文化班、拼音速成班的高中和大學使用，符合了美國AP中文課程的目標和基本要求。

　　本書是《雙雙中文教材》的第十三冊，適用於已學習掌握800個以上漢字的學生使用。中國神話傳說多產生於遠古的黃河流域，那時還沒有文字。中華民族的祖先在與自然搏鬥、求得生存的過程中戰勝了乾旱、洪水、疾病等重重困難，生存下來、發展起來，並創造了綿延至今的中華文明。本冊介紹了10篇美麗的神話傳說。學生們在進入這個神話世界時，會看到遠古時期中華民族的祖先與自然搏鬥時激動人心的場面，體會到中華民族勤勞勇敢、聰明智慧這些優良傳統源遠流長。

編者

課程設置

一年級	中文課本（第一冊）	中文課本（第二冊）	中文課本（第三冊）
二年級	中文課本（第四冊）	中文課本（第五冊）	中文課本（第六冊）
三年級	中文課本（第七冊）	中文課本（第八冊）	中文課本（第九冊）
四年級	中國成語故事		中國地理常識
五年級	中國古代故事		中國神話傳說
六年級	中國古代科學技術		中國文學欣賞
七年級	中國詩歌欣賞		中文科普閱讀
八年級	中國古代哲學		中國歷史（上）
九年級	中國歷史（下）		小說閱讀，中文SAT II
十年級	中文SAT II（強化班）		小說閱讀，中文SAT II 考試

目　錄

第一課　　盤古開天地 ……………………… 1

第二課　　女媧造人 ………………………… 8

第三課　　羿射九日 ………………………… 16

第四課　　嫦娥奔月 ………………………… 24

第五課　　神農嚐百草 ……………………… 31

第六課　　精衛填海 ………………………… 38

第七課　　夸父追日 ………………………… 44

第八課　　倉頡造字 ………………………… 50

第九課　　大禹治水 ………………………… 57

生字表　　…………………………………… 65

生詞表　　…………………………………… 67

第一課

盤古開天地

傳說遠古的時候，天和地沒有分開，黑暗的宇宙像一個大雞蛋，沒有太陽也沒有月亮。在這個大雞蛋裏睡著一個神，他就是盤古。

一萬八千年後，沉睡的盤古醒了。他睜眼一看，周圍很黑，悶得連氣都透不過來。他伸手四處摸，摸到了一把大斧頭。盤古就舉起大斧頭，朝黑暗砍去。"嘩huā啦啦"一聲巨響，大雞蛋破了！這時，輕又清的東西向上升，變成了藍天；重又濁的東西往下沉，變成了大地。

天和地分開了，盤古非常高興。但是天不夠高，他擔心天地又會合起來，就用頭頂著天，腳踩著地，像一根巨大的石柱，站在天地之間。盤古的身體每天都長高一丈。又過了一萬八千年，他的身子長到九萬里高，天地再也合不到一起了。盤古終于鬆了一口氣，這時的他感到非常疲勞。他抬頭望了望天空，又低頭看了看大地，笑了笑，便倒在地上，再也沒有醒過來。

　　盤古死時嘴裏呼出的氣，變成了風和雲；他的身體變成了大山；他的血液變成了江河湖海，肌肉變成了良田，筋脈變成了四通八達的道路；他的左眼變成了光輝的太陽，右眼變成了潔白的月亮，頭髮和鬍子變成了亮閃閃的星星；他皮膚上的汗毛變成了花草樹木；他的牙和骨頭變成礦物、石頭和珠寶；他的聲音變成了閃電和雷；就連他的汗水，也變成了雨水。

　　盤古開天闢地，又用自己的整個身體裝點世界，使世界變得十分美麗。

生詞

hēi àn 黑暗	dark	jī ròu 肌肉	muscle
yǔ zhòu 宇宙	universe	jīn mài 筋脈	tendons and arteries
fǔ tou 斧頭	ax	sì tōng bā dá 四通八達	extend in all directions
jù dà 巨大	huge	guāng huī 光輝	brilliant
zhuó 濁	turbid; muddy	jié bái 潔白	white
zhàng 丈	a unit of length	pí fū 皮膚	skin
sōng kǒu qì 鬆口氣	relax	kuàng wù 礦物	minerals
pí láo 疲勞	tired	kāi tiān pì dì 開天闢地	create the universe
hū chū 呼出	breath out	zhuāng diǎn 裝點	decorate
xuè yè 血液	blood		

聽寫

宇宙　血液　肌肉　光輝　潔白　巨大　呼出　皮膚

斧頭　黑暗　礦物　四通八達　*裝點　疲勞

注：標有*號的字詞為選做題，後同。

加偏旁再組詞

音—暗（黑暗）　　由—宙（宇宙）　　主—柱（柱子）

軍—輝（光輝）　　乎—呼（呼出）　　夜—液（血液）

父—斧（斧頭）　　皮—疲（疲勞）　　廣—礦（礦物）

詞語運用

盤古　盤子
盤古是傳說中開天闢地的英雄。

媽媽正在洗盤子。

頂著　一頂
下雨了，弟弟用頭頂著書包往家跑。

朋友送我一頂黃色的草帽。

筋脈　山脈
盤古死後，他的筋脈變成了道路。

天山山脈位于中國的新疆。

詞語解釋

四通八達——道路通向各方,交通方便。

例句:

北京的街道十分整齊,像個棋盤四通八達。

上海交通方便,道路四通八達。

閱讀

中國的姓氏(shì)

從盤古開天地以來,中國人到底有多少個姓氏呢?

早在五千年前,中國人就有了姓(xì)。那時是母系社會,人們只知道母親,不知道父親,每個人的姓都是跟著母親的,所以就連"姓"字,也是由"女"和"生"組成的。

傳說"炎"和"黃"兩大部落合併時,共有一百個氏族,因此把眾人叫作"百姓"。

中國有本古書叫《百家姓》,裏面一共收集了單姓、複姓共500多個,其中張、王、李是中國最大的三個姓。目前"李"姓是中國最大的姓,很可能也是全世界最大的姓了,單是姓李的就

有近一億人。另外張、王、李、趙、陳(chén)、楊(yáng)、吳、劉、黃、周這十個姓佔世界華人人口的40%，共約四億人。

中國各省都有一些比較集中的姓。如：廣東的梁(liáng)姓和羅(luó)姓，江蘇的徐(xú)姓和朱(zhū)姓，浙江的毛姓和沈(shěn)姓，湖北的胡姓，四川的何姓和鄧(dèng)姓，貴州的吳姓，雲南的楊(yáng)姓，寧夏的萬姓，新疆的馬姓，山東的孔姓，東北三省的于姓。科學家統計：從古到今中國人的姓氏已超過兩萬個(tǒng)。

問題

說一說你認識的中國人，他們姓什麼？請寫下來。

Pangu Creates the Universe

In the beginning, heaven and earth were united as a whole and the dark universe was like a huge egg without light from either the sun or the moon. A god, whose name was Pangu, was sleeping inside the egg.

After 18,000 years, Pangu awoke. He opened his eyes and saw nothing but darkness. Pangu found it suffocating. He groped about in the darkness and found a giant ax. Grabbing the ax tightly, Pangu swung at the darkness. With a thunderous crack, the huge egg split open. The clear and bright part ascended to form the blue sky; the muddy and heavy part sank to form the earth.

Pangu was overjoyed at separating heaven and earth. But the sky was not high enough and he

feared that the two would collapse back into each other, so he placed himself between them like a giant rock pillar, his head holding up the sky and his feet firmly upon the earth. Every day, Pangu grew taller by one zhang (about 3.3 meters) and after another 18,000 years, Pangu was 90,000 li tall. The heaven and the earth would never join togther again. Pangu was relieved but at the same time, he was extremely tired. He looked up to the sky, then looked down at the earth and smiled. Then he fell to the ground and never woke up again.

When Pangu died, his last breath turned into the wind and clouds. His body became huge mountains. His blood turned into rivers, lakes, and seas. His muscles became fertile land. His tendons and arteries turned into roads extending to all directions. His left eye turned into the brilliant sun and his right eye the bright moon. His hair and beard became twinkling stars. His body hair turned into trees, flowers, and grass. His teeth and bones became minerals, rocks, and precious stones. His voice turned into thunder and lightning. Even his sweat became raindrops.

Pangu created the universe and used his entire body to beautify the world, making it an exquisite place.

Surnames in China

Since the time Pangu created the universe, how many surnames have the Chinese people had?

The Chinese had surnames as early as 5,000 years ago. At that time, it was a matriarchal society based on maternal lineage. People could only know who their mothers were for sure, their fathers remaining largely a mystery. Therefore, they all used their mothers surnames. This is why the Chinese character for surname (姓) is composed of two parts-one meaning female(女) and the other meaning to give birth (生).

According to legend, two main tribes led by Emperor Yan and Emperor Huang merged, forming 100 clans and so people became known as *bai xing* (100 surnames) in China.

In an ancient Chinese book entitled *One Hundred Surnames* (*bai jia xing*), there are more than 500 one-character and two-character surnames. Among these, Zhang, Wang, and Li are the three most common surnames in China. Currently, there are about 100 million Chinese with the surname Li, making it the most common surname in China and most probably the entire world. The 10 most common surnames among the Chinese are Zhang, Wang, Li, Zhao, Chen, Yang, Wu, Liu, Huang, and Zhou. About 40%, or approximately 400 million, Chinese have these surnames.

In China, there is a tendency that people with particular surnames are concentrated in various provinces. For example, Liang and Luo are the two most common surnames in Guangdong, Xu and Zhu in Jiangsu, Mao and Shen in Zhejiang, Hu in Hubei, He and Deng in Sichuan, Wu in Guizhou, Yang in Yunnan, Wan in Ningxia, Ma in Xinjiang, Kong in Shandong, and Yu in three provinces in northeast China. According to statistics, there have been more than 20,000 surnames in China from ancient times till today.

第二課

女媧造人

盤古開闢了天地以後，天上有了日月星辰、白雲彩虹，地上有了山川湖泊、青草翠竹。鳥兒在花間鳴叫，魚兒在水中游玩，整個世界變得美麗而有生氣。這時一位偉大的女神女媧出現了。

女媧是一位善良的女神。一天黃昏，她獨自一人走在廣闊的原野上，感到十分孤獨。她想：要是天地間，能有許多像她這樣活潑(huó)的生命該多好啊！這時女媧走到一條小河邊，看見清清的河水中自己美麗的倒影。突然，她眼睛一亮，從河灘上抓起一把黃土，用水和成泥，不一會兒便捏出了一個和自己樣子差不多的小東西，女媧心裏十分高興。可是怎樣讓它動起來呢？女媧又朝他吹了口氣，這個泥捏的小東西居然能走路了。女媧又驚又喜，趕緊又捏起來。不一會兒，一群可愛的小娃娃出現了，圍著女媧跳著、笑著。女媧給這些小娃娃起了個名字，叫作"人"。

女媧不停地捏啊，造啊，沒有休息，她累極了。這時，她想出了一個辦法：把一根樹枝伸進河邊的泥裏，再往地上一甩，濺落的泥點都變成了人。這種方法雖然省事，但是甩出的人遠遠比

不上用手捏成的人那麼聰明和健壯。於是，從那時起，世界上就有了聰明人和笨人。

為什麼世界上有男人和女人呢？這是因為女媧在一些泥人兒身上吹了陽剛之氣，他們就變成了男人；在另一些泥人兒身上吹了陰柔之氣，她們就變成了女人。為了讓人類一代代地傳下去，女媧讓男人和女人相愛、結婚、生兒育女。

從此，人類就自由自在地生活在世界上。人們日出而作，日落而息，過著和平安寧的日子。

中國神話傳說

生詞

女媧 nǚ wā	a goddess in Chinese mythology	居然 jū rán	unexpectedly
星辰 xīngchén	stars	趕緊 gǎn jǐn	hastily
翠 cuì	green	休息 xiū xi	have a rest
鳴 míng	chirp	笨 bèn	stupid
黃昏 huáng hūn	dusk	陽剛 yánggāng	masculine
孤獨 gū dú	lonely	陰柔 yīn róu	feminine
活潑 huó pō	lively	人類 rén lèi	human kind
生命 shēngmìng	life	結婚 jié hūn	marry
倒影 dàoyǐng	reflection	生兒育女 shēng ér yù nǚ	give birth to children and nurture them
捏 niē	mold; knead with the fingers		
差不多 chà bu duō	similar	安寧 ān níng	peaceful

聽寫

黃昏　孤獨　活潑　生命　倒影　差不多　趕緊　星辰

笨　休息　人類　結婚　生兒育女　*捏　居然

比一比

孤（孤獨）　　　　　　昏（黃昏）
狐（狐狸）　　　　　　婚（結婚）

潑（活潑）　　　　　　辰（星辰）
發（出發）　　　　　　晨（早晨）

命｛生命／命令／拼命｝　　影｛倒影／電影／影子｝

居｛居然／居住／居民｝　　緊｛趕緊／緊張／抓緊｝

反義詞

聰明——愚笨　　陽剛——陰柔　　工作——休息

詞語運用

倒影　電影

女媧看見河水中自己美麗的倒影。

星期日，我們一家經常去看電影。

活潑　潑水

我有一個活潑可愛的小妹妹。

潑水節那天，人們互相潑水，真熱鬧。

朝

李白是唐朝偉大的詩人。

女媧朝泥人吹了一口氣。

詞語解釋

居然——沒想到。

例句：

我沒想到他這次考試居然得了第一。

這個泥捏的小東西居然能走路。

這麼厚的一本書你居然兩天就看完了。

我不敢相信，一條細細的蛇居然能把青蛙吞下去。

閱讀

女媧補bǔ天

女媧造了人，世界有了生氣，人類的生活一天天好起來。可是有一天水神共工和火神祝融打起仗來。他們從天上一直打到人間，打到了不周山腳下。結果火神勝了。失敗的水神一氣之下，用頭撞向不周山。不周山裂(liè)開了，支在天地之間的柱子斷了。天倒下了半邊，出現了一個大洞，地也裂開了。山林著起火來，洪(hóng)水從地下涌(yǒng)出，成千上萬的人被淹死了。

女媧看到這一切，心裏非常難受。她從大河中挑選出許多五彩石，把它們燒化成漿(jiāng)，用石漿把天上的洞補好。她又從一隻巨龜身上砍下四隻腳，當作四根柱子，把倒了的半邊天支了起來。

女媧把天補上了，地上的水也止住了，人類又重新過著安樂的生活。但是從這以後，天有點向西傾斜(qīng xié)，於是太陽、月亮和星星都很自然地落到西方；又因為地向東南傾斜，所以江河都向東流去；而五彩石變成了天上的彩雲，天空更美麗了。

小知識

女 媧

女媧是中國遠古神話傳說中創(chuàng)造人類的女神，創造萬物的偉大母親。

Goddess Nvwa Creates Men and Women

After Pangu created the universe, the sun, moon, stars, and clouds populated the sky and mountains, rivers, plants, birds, and fishes filled the earth. The world was teeming with life and filled with beauty. Then a great goddess named Nvwa appeared.

Nvwa was a kind goddess. One day at dusk, as she walked alone along the wild plains, she felt very lonely. Goddess Nvwa thought it would be nice if there were other creatures like herself in the universe. At this moment, she walked to a river and saw her own reflection in the water. Suddenly she had an idea. She grasped a handful of soil from the river bed and mixed it with water. Using the clay, she molded a small model of herself and blew life into it. The little clay creature began to move. Delighted, Goddess Nvwa made more of them and was soon surrounded by a group of adorable little creatures who were jumping about and laughing. Goddess Nvwa named them human beings.

The goddess continued to mold more human beings. With no time to rest, she soon grew tired.

Then she had another idea. Taking a tree branch, she dipped it into the mud beside the river and flicked the muddy branch against the ground. Blobs of mud landed on the ground; each of these blobs turned into a human being. This method was efficient but the human beings formed this way were not as clever and strong as those kneaded by the goddess herself. This explains why there are clever people and foolish ones in the world.

Why are there men and women in the world? This is because Goddess Nvwa blew masculine breath into some clay figures and they turned into men; she blew feminine breath into others and they became women. In order that human beings populate and continue through generation after generation, the goddess gave men and women the ability to fall in love, marry, and give birth to more children.

From then on, human beings lived freely on earth. They worked when the sun rose and rested when the sun set, and led happy and peaceful lives.

Goddess Nvwa Mends the Sky

Since Goddess Nvwa created human beings, the world became full of life and men担 lives improved gradually. But one day, Gonggong (the God of Water) and Zhurong (the God of Fire) had a fight. They fought all the way from heaven to earth. Finally, Zhurong won. The defeated Gonggong was so angry that he struck his head against Mount Buzhou, a pillar holding up the sky. The pillar collapsed. Half of the sky fell in and a big hole appeared in the sky. The earth cracked open. Forests went up in flames. Floodwaters sprouted from beneath the earth and drowned tens of thousands of people.

Goddess Nvwa was grieved to see such suffering. She chose a pile of rocks of five different colors from the river and melted them into magma to patch the hole in the sky. Then she cut off the four legs of a giant tortoise and used them to support the fallen part of the sky.

With the sky patched up and the floodwaters stopped, people lived happily again. But the sky was no longer even as before and tilted to the west. This is why the sun, the moon, and all the stars naturally go down to the west. In addition, since the land tilted to the southeast, all the rivers began to flow eastward to the sea. The rocks of five colors also transformed into colorful clouds, making the sky even more beautiful than before.

中國神話傳說

第三課

羿^{yì}射九日

很久以前，天空突然出現了十個太陽。這十個太陽就是天帝的十個兒子。天帝讓他們一天一個輪流出去到人間工作。可是他們不聽話，總是貪玩，一起出來。十個太陽把草木曬枯，河水曬乾；人們也熱得難受，喘不上氣來。

天帝看到他的十個兒子這樣胡鬧，十分生氣，就叫天神"羿"去教訓教訓他們。羿帶著天帝給他的神弓、神箭，與妻子嫦娥一起來到了人間。

羿到了人間，先是對著太陽舉起弓箭來裝裝樣子，想嚇唬嚇唬那十個太陽。可是，十個太陽根本沒把羿放在眼裏，還是一起出來，一起回去，故意和人們搗亂。再這樣下去人們就無法生活了。羿十分生氣，舉起神弓神箭，對準天上的太陽，一箭射了過去。只聽空中一聲巨響，火光亂閃，金色的羽毛四下飄落；又聽"撲"的一聲，一個金色大火球落在地上。人們一看，是一隻巨大的金黃色三足烏鴉。再看看天上，只剩下九個太陽了，天氣也

變得涼快了一些。人們高興得拍手歡呼起來，大聲叫道："射得好，再射！"

羿向著天上東一個西一個正在驚慌逃跑的太陽連連射去。一時間，金色的羽毛紛紛飄下，金黃色的三足烏鴉一隻接一隻地落到了地上。當天上只剩下一個太陽的時候，人們突然想起有太陽才有白天，有太陽才有溫暖，禾苗才能生長。他們要求羿留下最後一個太陽。從此天上就只有一個太陽了。

羿以為自己立了大功，高高興興地返回天上去見天帝。可是他連做夢也沒有想到，天帝十分生氣，對他說："好一個神射手，好一個大英雄！你把我的九個兒子都殺了。好吧，既然人們喜歡你，你就留在他們中間好了。

從此以後，你和嫦娥就到人間去吧，不要再回到天上來了。"

羿悶悶不樂地回到家中，告訴妻子這個消息。當知道他們不能回到天上的時候，嫦娥便傷心地哭起來。她想到自己原本是天上的女神，如今卻成了凡人，而凡人遲早是會死的，就天天生氣，鬧著要羿想辦法去找長生不老藥。羿只好到處去找仙藥。

生詞

lún liú 輪流	take turns	liáng kuai 涼快	cool
shài kū 曬枯	sunbaked	huān hū 歡呼	cheer
nán shòu 難受	uncomfortable; unwell	jīng huāng 驚慌	panic-stricken
hú nào 胡鬧	make trouble; do mischief	yāo qiú 要求	ask; request
cháng é 嫦娥	a goddess in Chinese mythology	fǎn huí 返回	return
xià hu 嚇唬	frighten	yīngxióng 英雄	hero
dǎo luàn 搗亂	make trouble	mènmèn bú lè 悶悶不樂	glum
shèng xià 剩下	be left (over); remain	fán rén 凡人	mortal being

聽寫

輪流　曬枯　返回　剩下　要求　歡呼　嚇唬　難受　驚慌

英雄　凡人　*悶悶不樂

比一比

相 { 相傳 / 相信 / 相互

輪 { 輪流 / 車輪 / 輪到

{ 島（島嶼） / 搗（搗亂）

曬 { 曬枯 / 曬乾 / 曬太陽

歡 { 歡呼 / 歡迎 / 喜歡

反義詞

凡人──神仙　　　悶悶不樂──快快樂樂

涼快──炎熱

多音字

要 yào　　　要 yāo

要是 yào　　　要求 yāo

詞詞運用

輪流　車輪

我和哥哥每天輪流洗碗。

這輛汽車的車輪壞了。

胡鬧　熱鬧

弟弟總愛胡鬧，用糖餵小魚。

上海是一個熱鬧的大城市。

加偏旁再組詞

島—搗（搗亂）　　　反—返（返回）

古—枯（乾枯）　　　虎—唬（嚇唬）

麗—曬（曬乾）　　　京—涼（涼快）

神射手——羿

一次，羿上山打獵。一位年輕獵人走上來說："聽說你是神箭手，我們能不能比比射箭？"羿答應了。于是獵人對羿射出一支箭。羿不慌不忙搭好箭迎頭射去。兩支箭空中相碰，"嚓啷"一聲都落在地上。獵人一連射出九支箭，都被羿用箭擋在空中。這時羿的箭用完了，可是又有一支箭飛來，羿連忙張開嘴，一下子咬住箭頭，假裝倒在地上。獵人以為羿被射中了，哪知羿把嘴裏的箭吐出來迅速搭在弓上，對著獵人喊道："小心，看箭！"一箭射去，把獵人的帽子射掉了。獵人馬上拜倒在地，說："我的箭法不如你，願拜你為師。"

羿收他做了徒弟，對他說："要想學射箭，先得學會不眨眼睛。"獵人回家後看見妻子在織布，就盯著織布機的梭子看。梭子動他眼睛不動。一直練到就是有蚊蟲從他眼前飛過，他也不會眨一眨眼。

羿見他有長進，又教他說："還要練眼力，要練到能把很小的東西看成大東西才行。"于是獵人抓了一隻小蟲挂在窗戶上，天天盯著它看。不久他覺得小蟲在他眼中已經變得像車輪一樣大了。羿這才點點頭，把自己射箭的技術教給了這位年輕獵人。後來他和羿射得一樣好，也成了一名神箭手。

Yi Shoots Down Nine Suns

  A long time ago, 10 suns suddenly appeared in the sky. These were actually the 10 sons of the Celestial Ruler, who had ordered them to each take turns to rise and give the world light every morning. But the sons were disobedient and always rose together for fun. The heat from the 10 suns caused plants to shrivel and rivers to dry. People suffered greatly in the unbearable heat.

  The Celestial Ruler became angry upon seeing his sons' mischief. He instructed God Yi to teach them a lesson. Yi accepted the supernal bow and arrows from the Celestial Ruler, and descended to earth with his wife, Chang'e.

  At the beginning, Yi lifted his bow and pretended to take aim at the suns, hoping to frighten them. But the 10 suns did not pay him any attention; they continued their mischief by rising and setting together. If this persisted, the people would never live. Angered by the 10 suns' misdeeds, Yi raised his supernal bow and arrow, aimed at one sun in the sky and released the bowstring. A loud noise was heard and with golden feathers fluttering in the air, a huge golden fireball landed on the ground with a thud. The people gathered around it and saw a giant golden crow with three feet lying on the ground. Looking up at the sky, they counted nine suns left. It was also a little cooler than before. The crowd applauded and cheered, "Good job! Shoot again!"

  With the crowd cheering, Yi pointed his arrows at the remaining nine suns that were now scattering in panic in all directions. Soon, golden feathers were drifting down and one by one, the golden crows fell to the ground. At last, only one sun remained in the sky. Realizing that the sun gave light and warmth, without which plants could not grow. the people pleaded with Yi to spare the last sun. From then on, there was only one sun in the sky.

  Thinking that he had accomplished the task entrusted to him, Yi returned to heaven happily. He never dreamed that the Celestial Ruler would be furious at him. The Celestial Ruler said, "What a great marksman, what a great hero. You've killed nine of my sons! Since you are so popular among mortals, you shall remain with them on earth. You and your wife shall never return to the celestial palace again."

Yi returned home glumly and told his wife the news. When Chang 'e realized that they would never be able to return to the celestial world, she cried miserably. Whenever she thought about the fact that she used to be a goddess but has now become a mortal being and would one day die, she would become upset and insist that Yi find elixirs so that they can live forever and never grow old. Left with no choice, Yi searched for elixirs everywhere he went.

Yi—the Marksman

One day, Yi went hunting in the mountains. A young hunter came up to him and said, "I have heard that you are a great marksman. Shall we have a competition?" Yi agreed. The hunter then shot an arrow at Yi. Calmly, Yi took out his arrow, put it on the bow and pulled back the bowstring. He released the bowstring and shot the young hunter's arrow down. One by one, the hunter shot nine arrows at Yi but all were stopped by Yi's arrows. Yi had run out of arrows when the hunter shot once more at him. Yi immediately opened his mouth and bit the arrowhead before pretending to fall onto the ground. The hunter thought Yi had been shot, but Yi then quickly put the arrow in his mouth on the bow and aimed at the hunter, yelling, "Look out!" The cap on the hunter's head was subsequently shot down. The hunter fell to the ground, saying, "My archery skills are inferior to yours. Please be my master."

Yi accepted him as his disciple and said to him, "To learn to be an archery master, first you have to learn not to blink." Upon returning home, the young hunter found his wife weaving. He stared at the pedals of the weaving machine and tried hard not to blink while the pedals moved back and forth. The young hunter continued practicing until he succeeded in not blinking even when mosquitoes flew past his eyes.

Seeing the young hunter's progress, Yi was satisfied and told him, "Now you must practice your focus. You must train hard until you can look at a small object and see it growing bigger. The young hunter then caught a louse and hung it before the window, staring at it day after day. Before long, he felt that when he looked at the louse, he was seeing a big cartwheel. It was only then Yi began teaching him the art of archery. Soon, the young hunter could shoot as well as Yi and became a marksman like his master.

第四課

嫦娥奔月

　　崑崙山上住著一個神仙，叫西王母。羿聽說她那兒藏著長生不老藥，就決定去找她。西王母非常同情這位英雄，就給了他一包藥，並對他說："這就是長生不老藥。你和嫦娥兩個人分著吃

這包藥，可以都長生不老。要是一個人吃了全部的藥，還能升天成神。"

羿帶著長生不老藥高高興興地回到家裏，準備挑個好日子和嫦娥一同把藥吃了。羿不想上天，他覺得天上並不比人間好。嫦娥可不這麼想，她還是希望當神仙。自從羿射死了九個太陽以後，她一直怨恨著羿。一天夜裏，嫦娥看著沉睡的丈夫，心想：如果吃了這包藥，就能上天成神，我為什麼不自己吃呢？羿是自作自受，我並沒有射太陽，為什麼天帝要罰我和他一起留在人間呢？於是她悄悄把藥拿出來，一個人全吃了。突然，她的腳漸漸離開了地面，身子輕輕地飄起來，飄出窗口，朝天上飛去。不過，她不敢回天庭，怕眾神說她背棄丈夫。她決定到月宮去住一住。

讓嫦娥失望的是，月宮非常冷清，只有一隻玉兔，一棵桂花樹和一個被罰砍桂樹的吳剛。嫦娥很後悔，她一下子想起了羿的那麼多好處，很想返回人間，可是藥已經吃了，哪裏還能回得去？她只能永遠生活在冷冷清清的月宮裏，思念著她的丈夫。

生詞

jué dìng 決定	decide	bèi qì 背棄	abandon; betray
tóng qíng 同情	sympathize	shī wàng 失望	disappointed
xī wàng 希望	hope	lěng qīng 冷清	cold and cheerless
yuàn hèn 怨恨	hate; resent	guì huā 桂花	osmanthus
zì zuò zì shòu 自作自受	suffer from one's own actions	hòu huǐ 後悔	regret
fá 罰	punish	sī niàn 思念	miss
jiàn jiàn 漸漸	gradually		

聽寫

同情　漸漸　決定　罰　希望　思念

失望　後悔　*自作自受　怨恨

比一比

{ 崑（崑崙山）
　昆（昆蟲）

{ 恨（怨恨）
　很（很多）

受 { 自作自受 / 受罰 / 受苦 }　　母（母親　父母） { 每（每天　每次） / 悔（後悔　悔恨） }

詞語運用

希望　失望

我一直希望有一臺筆記本電腦。

小華游泳比賽沒得到第一名，她感到很失望。

反義詞

漸漸——突然　　愛——恨　　冷清——熱鬧

詞語解釋

自作自受——自己做了錯事，自己受罰。

例句：

小明玩火把手指燒傷了，真是自作自受。

嫦娥偷吃仙藥，飛上寂寞的月宮，真是自作自受。

中秋節

宋愷琦

在中國的傳統節日裏，除了春節這個喜慶大節日以外，中秋節是第二個重要的節日。中秋節在每年農曆的八月十五日，是全家團圓的日子。兒女們要回家看父母，並一起吃晚飯、賞月亮，特別要一起吃月餅。

中秋的月餅是圓的，代表著團團圓圓。八月十五的月亮又大又圓，代表著全家平安、幸福。

兩年前，我們全家去了杭州，正好碰上過中秋節。那天爺爺奶奶帶我們去西湖邊一個名叫"平湖秋月"的亭子吃夜宵。那晚，月亮圓圓的、亮亮的，像一個銀盤挂在天上。西湖裏倒映著的月亮也是又大又圓，非常美。我吃了一個甜月餅，心裏甜甜的。

今年中秋節，我們提前兩天，在周末請了一些朋友到家裏來，一起過節。爸爸媽媽做了許多中國菜，有雞、鴨、蝦、魚和肉，又買了中國的月餅，一起品嚐。我們也賞

張羅蘊 畫

了月，那天月亮也是又圓又亮的，跟中國的月亮一樣美。媽媽說再過兩天就更圓了。可惜中秋節那天下雨了，我們沒看見月亮。爸爸媽媽說每到中秋節的時候就會特別想他們的父母——我的爺爺、奶奶、外公和外婆。

Chang'e Flies to the Moon

There lived a celestial goddess named Xiwangmu (Queen Mother of the West) on the Kunlun Mountain. Having learned that she possessed the elixir of life, Yi decided to travel to the mountain where the Queen Mother lived. The Queen Mother sympathized with him and gave him a pack of the elixir. She said, "This is enough for you and Chang'e to live forever. If only one of you finishes all the pills, he or she will ascend to heaven and become immortal."

Yi went home happily with the elixir, planning to choose an auspicious date to take the pills together with his wife. Unlike Chang'e who yearned to be an immortal again, Yi was content with life on earth; he did not want to go back to the celestial palace. In fact, Chang'e kept resenting Yi, since he shot down nine suns. One night, as Chang'e looked at her sleeping husband, she thought, "If I eat all of these pills, I will be a goddess again. Why shouldn't I eat them? It was all Yi's fault and why should I be punished for his deeds? I didn't shoot down the suns." Then she took out the pills and swallowed them all. All of a sudden, her feet left the ground and she flew out of the window and up to the sky. Fearing that the other gods and goddesses would condemn her for betraying her husband, Chang'e did not dare to return to the celestial palace. Instead, she flew directly to the moon.

Chang'e was disappointed at finding that the moon palace was cold and cheerless. There was only one jade rabbit, one sweet osmanthus tree, and a woodcutter named Wugang who was condemned to cutting trees there. Chang'e began to regret betraying her husband. She remembered Yi's virtues and wanted to go back to him. But because she had already eaten the elixir of life, it was impossible for her to return to earth. Chang'e lived in the desolate moon palace, missing her husband forever.

The Mid-Autumn Festival

Among traditional Chinese holidays, the Mid-Autumn Festival is one of the most important holidays in the Chinese lunar calendar, second only to the Chinese Lunar New Year. It falls on the 15th day of the 8th lunar month of the Chinese lunar calendar and is a day for family reunion. Children return

home to visit their parents, have dinner together, and admire the full moon while sharing mooncakes.

Mooncakes are round, which represents reunion. The moon is also at its fullest and brightest on this day, which signifies peace and happiness for the entire family.

Two years ago, my family traveled to Hangzhou during the Mid-Autumn Festival. That day, my grandparents took us out for supper at "Autumn Moon over the Calm Lake", a pavilion beside the West Lake. The moon was round and bright that night, like a silver plate hanging in the sky. The reflection of the moon in the West Lake was also full and beautiful. As I ate the sweet mooncake, I felt happiness in my heart.

This year, we celebrated the Mid-Autumn Festival two days in advance. We invited some friends home for the celebration over the weekend. My parents cooked a lot of Chinese dishes; there was chicken, duck, shrimp, fish, and pork. We also shared Chinese mooncakes while admiring the moon. That night, the moon was also full and bright like that in China. Mother said the moon would be at its fullest two days later. But it rained on the day of the Mid-Autumn Festival and we did not see the moon. My parents said it was during this holiday season that they will miss their parents, my grandparents, in China.

第五課

神農嘗百草

傳說炎帝是一個善良的神。他長得非常奇怪：全身都是透明的，一眼就能看見心肝等五髒。

那時候，人們只會採野果和種子吃。可是人越來越多，能吃的東西卻越來越少，人們經常挨餓。炎帝看到後，就教人們種五穀雜糧，又讓太陽照著禾苗，給禾苗光和熱。從此，人們就有吃的和穿的了。人們感謝炎帝，稱他為"神農"。

人們有了吃和穿，很高興。可是人們生病的時候，卻一點辦法也沒有。有的人肚子疼，有的人頭暈，有的人吐，生病的人難受極了。神農看見了，就想給人們治病，可是給病人吃什麼藥呢？這可難住了神農。他想了整整一天一夜，最後決定自己把樹木、花草嘗遍，知道哪些是草藥，證明它們有用，然後再給病人吃。這樣人們才不會吃錯藥。

由於神農的身子是透明的，他嘗了草以後就可以看見藥走到哪裏，身體哪兒有什麼變化。如果中(zhòng)了毒，他就趕緊嘗試別的花草，看看哪種花草可以解毒。這樣他就知道哪些花草可以解毒、哪些花草可以治病。他嚐遍了所有能找到的植物。有時他一天就中毒十二次，可他也明白了中毒的部位，並找到了解救的藥方。

一年又一年，神農救了無數人的生命。可是有一次，他不幸嚐了一種毒性很強的斷腸草，眼看著腸子一寸寸地爛掉，竟然找不到解救的藥方。

人們都為神農著急，但是也沒有辦法救活他。神農為給人們治病，獻出了自己的生命。

人們世世代代懷念神農。至今還有許多中藥店都挂著神農的畫像。聽說山西太原的神釜
gāng
岡，還有一隻神農做藥用過的鼎呢。

第五課

生詞

cháng 嚐	taste	jiě dú 解毒	detoxify; detoxicate
yán dì 炎帝	Yan Di (a legendary ruler in the mythology of ancient China)	suǒ yǒu 所有	all
		jiě jiù 解救	save; rescue
		yào fāng 藥方	medical prescription
tòu míng 透明	transparent	bú xìng 不幸	unfortunate
xīn gān 心肝	heart and liver	cháng zi 腸子	intestines
wǔ zàng 五臟	five internal organs	cùn 寸	a unit of length
ái è 挨餓	suffer from hunger	jìng rán 竟然	unexpectedly
wǔ gǔ zá liáng 五穀雜糧	grains	xiàn chū 獻出	sacrifice
tóu yūn 頭暈	dizzy; giddy	shì dài 世代	for generations
tù 吐	vomit	huáiniàn 懷念	cherish the memory of
zhèngmíng 證明	prove	dǐng 鼎	an ancient cooking vessel
cháng shì 嘗試	try		

聽寫

嘗試　炎帝　透明　心肝　五臟　五穀雜糧　吐　不幸

所有的　世代　證明　腸子　解毒　*竟然

比一比

炎 { 炎帝 / 炎熱 }　　透 { 透明 / 透氣 }　　雜 { 雜糧 / 複雜 }

解 { 解毒 / 解開 }　　決 { 決心 / 決定 }　　爛 { 爛掉 / 破爛 }

多音字

教(jiāo) { 教課 / 教書 }　　教(jiào) { 教師 / 教室 }

中(zhòng) 中毒(zhòng)　　中(zhōng) 中華(zhōng)

同音字

嚐嚐　常常　長長

請你嚐嚐我做的這道菜。

李小光常常去圖書館看書。

張華穿了一條長長的裙(qún)子。

詞語解釋

竟然——表示沒想到，很吃驚。

例句：

這麼重要的消息你竟然不知道？

他竟然敢一個人在深海游泳。

幾年不見，他竟然長得比他爸爸還高了。

閱讀

針灸(jiǔ)的起源

針灸在中國有幾千年的歷史了。針灸包括兩種古老的治病方法：針法和灸法。針法是用針刺入人體的穴(xué)位治病；灸法是用燒著的艾(ài)草在穴位上熱烤來治病。

針刺

遠古時期，有時人們被尖硬的石頭或帶刺的植物扎(zhā)了身體某(mǒu)個部位，原來的一些病痛反倒好些了。這樣的情況多了，便引起了人們的注意。後來，人們磨製出砭(biān)石刺入身體來治病。砭石也被稱為針石，是最早的"針"。

灸 法

原始人發現，在他們烤火取暖時，身體被火熱烤以後會有舒(shū)服的感覺，原來的一些病痛（如關節炎等）也減輕了。由于艾草的葉子容易燃燒，氣味芳(fāng)香，容易加工，人們就用艾葉作燃料(liào)，對身體一些部位進行熱烤。灸法也就流傳開了。

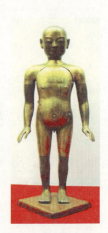

English Translation

Shennong Tastes Hundreds of Herbs

Legend has it that there was a benevolent god named Yan Di. Yan Di had a strange appearance as his body was transparent and his internal organs were clearly visible to others.

At that time, people ate wild fruit and seeds. However, as the population multiplied, food supply became scarce and people often went hungry. Upon seeing this, Yan Di began teaching people how to cultivate grains as food. He let the sun shine on the crops, thereby providing light and heat for the plants. From then on, people had enough food to eat and clothes to keep them warm. They were grateful to Yan Di and called him Shennong, the god of farming.

With their needs taken care of, people lived happily. But when they fell ill, they became helpless. Some had stomachaches, some suffered from headaches and some vomited. They became miserable. Shennong wished to cure them but did not know what kinds of herbs he should prescribe. He was stumped and spent a day and night pondering over the issue. Finally, he decided to personally taste all kinds of herbs to test their medicinal value before prescribing them to the sick so that people would not be take the wrong medication.

Thanks to his transparent body, Shennong could see the changes to his body after he ate the herbs. If he was poisoned, he would quickly try other herbs to find the antidote. In this way, he discovered which herbs were antidotal in nature and which could cure illnesses. Shennong tasted all the herbs he found. There were times when he was poisoned as many as 12 times in a span of one day. But it was in this manner that he discovered the exact part of the body that was poisoned and the antidote to counteract the poisonous effect.

As time passed, Shennong saved numerous lives. Unfortunately, one day, he tasted an extremely toxic herb. He watched his own intestines rot inch by inch and could not find the antidote. Everyone worried for him, but could not find any way to save him. In the course of saving lives, Shennong sacrificed his own.

Generations went by but people still remember Shennong. Even till today, his portrait can be seen hanging in many Chinese pharmacies. A *ding* (an ancient cooking vessel) that is believed to have been used by him is preserved at the Shenfu Gang of Taiyuan, Shanxi Province.

The Origin of Acupuncture and Moxibustion

Acupuncture and moxibustion have a long history in China. Both are ancient therapeutic methods that are used to treat diseases. Acupuncture is a technique of inserting needles into acupuncture points in the body while moxibustion is a form of therapy that uses ignited moxa to warm acupuncture points.

Acupuncture

In ancient times, there were instances when people got pierced by sharp stones or prickly plants and experienced relief from certain pains or illnesses that they were originally suffering from. Gradually, this phenomenon started to attract attention. People began to make sharp pointed rocks and inserted these into certain sections of their bodies to treat illnesses. These pointed rocks are also known as stone needles and are known as the earliest "needles".

Moxibustion

Ancient people discovered that when they warmed themselves by the fire, the heat not only produced a comfortable sensation, it also relieved them of certain pains (for example, arthritis). Because moxa leaves are easily processed and ignited, and it has a pleasant fragrance, people eventually chose it as the substance to warm certain parts of the body. Since then, moxibustion has increased in popularity.

第六課

精衛填海

遠古的時候，炎帝有一位愛女，名叫女娃。女娃常常去東海邊遊玩，和仙女一起游水。不料有一次游到深海，風大浪急，女娃被海水淹沒了，再也沒有回來。炎帝聽到後，悲痛萬分，於是下令：不許百姓出海打魚，不許遠游。

女娃死後變成了一隻小鳥，白嘴、紅腳、頭上有彩色的羽毛。

一天，炎帝在樹林中打獵，一隻美麗的小鳥繞著他的頭飛來飛去，悲哀地叫著："精——衛，精——衛！"炎帝舉弓要射小鳥，一位道士跑來告訴炎帝說："這小鳥是您的女兒女

娃變的！"炎帝心中一驚，放下弓箭，心像撕裂了一樣，忍不住淚如雨下，久久不能平靜。許久之後，炎帝才說："就給小鳥取個名字叫'精衛'吧！"精衛在父親的頭頂上來回飛著，久久不肯離去。炎帝望著"精衛"，悲傷地唱道：

精衛鳴兮（xī），天地動容！

山木翠兮，人為魚蟲！

嬌女不能言兮，父至悲痛！

海何以不平兮，波濤洶湧！

願子孫後代兮，勿入海中！

願吾民族兮，永以大陸為榮！

歌的意思是：

精衛鳥在聲聲哀叫，天地也被感動了。

山林還是那樣蒼翠啊，我女兒卻淹沒在海中！

嬌女再也無法說話了，父親是多麼地悲痛！

大海為什麼不能被填平呢！波浪依然洶湧！

但願我的子孫後代呀，萬萬不要掉入海中！

但願我的民族啊，永遠讚美帶給人們安全的大陸！

精衛聽到父親"海何以不平"的歌詞，下決心填平大海！於是，不管春夏秋冬，颱風下雨，精衛鳥每天都叼小樹枝、小石塊

丟到大海裏。雖然木石一下就被浪濤沖走了，但是她還是一刻不停地飛來飛去把石子不斷地投進海裏。大海奪去了她年輕的生命，為了讓其他孩子不再被淹死，她發誓要填平大海。

直到今天，精衛鳥還在不停地叼石子填海。

生詞

tián 填	fill up	wú 吾	I (in ancient Chinese)
bú liào 不料	unexpectedly	yǐ……wéi róng 以……為榮	be glorified because of...
bēi tòng 悲痛	sorrowful; grieved	cāng cuì 蒼翠	lush
bēi āi 悲哀	doleful	yī rán 依然	still
sī liè 撕裂	tear	dàn yuàn 但願	wish; desire
qǔ míng 取名	give a name	zàn měi 讚美	admire; praise
bù kěn 不肯	be unwilling to	jué xīn 決心	be determined to
jiāo nǚ 嬌女	beloved daughter	yí kè bù tíng 一刻不停	ceaselessly
zhì 至	extremely	tóu 投	throw
bō tāo xiōng yǒng 波濤洶湧	turbulent waves	fā shì 發誓	swear; vow
wù 勿	no; not		

聽寫

不料　不肯　填平　勿　悲哀　依然　取名

決心　但願　榮　嬌女　投　*發誓　讚美

比一比

填 { 填海 / 填表

悲 { 悲伤 / 悲痛

讚 { 讚美 / 讚同

肯 { 不肯 / 肯定

決 { 決定 / 決心

投 { 投進 / 投入

詞語運用

不料

我們原來要去爬山，不料下雨了，只好待在家裏。

同學們去看電影，不料票賣完了，結果沒有看成。

勿

請勿吸煙！

不肯

妹妹生病了又不肯吃藥，媽媽很著急。

弟弟只喜歡吃肉，不肯吃菜，結果越長越胖。

決心

我決心每天游泳30分鐘。

小明決心每天用中文寫日記。

詞語解釋

不料——事先沒有想到。

不斷——接連，不停止。

小知識

精衛鳥

精衛是海邊一種黑色的小鳥，頭上的羽毛有花紋(wén)，白嘴紅爪。這種小鳥有個奇特的習性，就是經常把岸上的小樹枝、小石塊用嘴叼著丟到大海裏。

Jingwei Filling Up the Sea

Long ago, there was an emperor named Yan Di and he had a beloved daughter whose name was Nvwa. Princess Nvwa often went swimming in the East Sea with the fairy maidens. On one occasion, when she was swimming in the deep sea, she encountered strong winds and turbulent waves. Princess Nvwa drowned and never returned. Yan Di was heartbroken upon hearing the news. He issued an order that no one was allowed to go fishing in the sea or swim far out to sea again.

After Princess Nvwa died, her spirit transformed into a small bird with a white beak, red feet, and had multicolored feathers on its head.

One day, Yan Di went hunting in the forest. A beautiful bird hovered above him, chirping, "Jingwei, Jingwei." Yan Di lifted his bow and was about to shoot the bird when a Taoist priest came running to him, saying, "This bird is really Princess Nvwa, your daughter!" Startled, Yan Di lowered his bow. Feeling very grieved, tears began streaming down his face. When he finally regained his composure, he said, "Let's name the bird 'Jingwei.'" Jingwei circled above her father for a long time. As Yan Di looked at the bird, he began to sing sadly:

At your crying, Jingwei, both heaven and earth are moved.

The forest remains ever so green, but my dear daughter has drowned in the sea.

My dear girl would never speak with me again, oh how sad that is for a father!

Why can't the sea be filled up? The waves continue to surge.

May all my descendents never ever fall into the sea!

May all my people forever praise the safe land!

Upon hearing her father's song, Jingwei was determined to fill up the sea. Since then, regardless of the season or the weather, Jingwei would bring small twigs and pebbles and drop them into the sea each day. Although the twigs and pebbles would be immediately washed away by the waves, she continued to throw them into the sea. The sea had taken away her young life and in order that no other young lives should be lost to it, she vowed to fill up the ocean.

To this day, Jingwei continues to diligently fill the sea with pebbles.

第七課

夸父追日

在遠古的中國北方有一個叫夸父的人。他又高又大,很有力氣,而且跑得飛快。

夸父天天到山中打獵。一天,他看見一隻野兔,就拿石頭打過去,不料打歪了,野兔東跑西跳,夸父抓不著它。這樣,他越追越遠,直到天色已晚,還沒有追上這隻野兔。夸父跑累了,坐在山邊的石頭上休息。他抬眼望去,只見太陽快要落到西山後面。夸父想:要是能把太陽捉住,固定在天空,讓大地永遠是一

片光明，沒有黑暗，那該多好啊！

這樣想著，夸父站了起來，邁開大步向著太陽落下的地方跑去。一會兒的工夫，他已經跑出幾千里地，來到禺谷。這禺谷，是太陽每天休息的地方。夸父一看，一團巨大的紅紅的火球就在他的頭頂上，那麼輝煌、光明，他歡喜極了。

突然，夸父感到一陣難忍的口渴，他便伏下身子，一口氣把黃河和渭河的水都喝乾了。可是他還是渴得要命，只好又向北面跑去。夸父知道，那裏有一個叫"瀚海"的大湖，大湖裏的水足夠他喝的。可是，路途太遙遠了，夸父又渴又累，還沒跑到瀚海，就死在了中途。

巨人夸父像一座山似的倒下，他看了看正在落下去的太陽，長嘆一聲，使出全身的力氣，把手裏的木杖往前面一拋，便停止了呼吸。

當太陽再一次從東方升起，萬道金光照耀大地的時候，人們才發現，昨天倒在原野上的巨人夸父不見了，那裏出現了一座大山。山腳下有一片桃林。桃樹上長著又大又紅的桃子。人們知道，這座山就是夸父的化身，那桃林是夸父的手杖變的，一顆顆鮮桃是夸父留給人們的，使人們尋求光明時不再口渴，能把光明帶給人間。

生詞

wāi 歪	askew; tilted	zhōng tú 中途	midway
gù dìng 固定	fix	xiàng shì de 像……似的	look like
mài kāi 邁開	take (a step)	mù zhàng 木杖	wooden club
huī huáng 輝煌	splendent; bright	pāo 拋	fling; throw
fú xià 伏下	bend over	hū xī 呼吸	breath
zú gòu 足夠	enough	zhào yào 照耀	shine; blaze
lù tú 路途	journey	xún qiú 尋求	seek
yáo yuǎn 遙遠	faraway; remote		

聽寫

遙遠　歪　固定　邁開　足夠　尋求　照耀

路途　像……似的　呼吸　*輝煌

比一比

夠 { 不夠 / 足夠 }　　呼 { 歡呼 / 呼吸 }　　途 { 路途 / 中途 }　　耀 { 照耀 / 誇耀 }

詞語運用

永遠　遙遠

太陽永遠從東方升起。

爸爸在遙遠的南極工作。

尋求

人們不斷地尋求醫治癌(zhèng)症的辦法。

保護動物組織向民眾尋求幫助。

（像）……似的

小妹妹的臉紅得像個小蘋果似的。

劉洋飛似的跑了過來。

閱讀

五彩池

神話傳說中天上有一個五彩池。可是在四川的藏(cáng)龍山，滿山坡的五彩池大大小小多得數不清。這些五彩池大的不足一畝(mǔ)，水深不到三米；小的呢，只有盤子大小，水淺(qiǎn)得用手可以摸到池底。池子的邊是金黃色的，像金色的帶子把池子圍成各種形狀：有的像葫蘆(hú lu)，有的像月牙，有的像盛開的蓮花……

　　站在山上，向下望去，滿山坡的水池在日光下，閃著紅、黃、綠、藍等各種色彩。讓人奇怪的是，這些彩池雖然互相連接，但每池水的顏色却各不相同。有的上邊的池水是咖(kā)啡(fēi)色，可是一流入下邊的池中，就變成了黃色；有的左邊的池水是湖藍色，一流進右邊的池中，却變成了綠色；有的一個水池會出現多種色彩。如果把各池的水舀(yǎo)起來一看，却又跟普通清水一樣，什麼顏色也没有。這是怎麼一回事呢？原來池底長著許多石筍，而這些石筍表面又有一層細細的石粉，在日光的照射下，池底就像

一面面高低不平的反光鏡，顯出各種美麗的顏色，使五彩池看起來非常神奇。

Kuafu Chases after the Sun

　　Once upon a time, there lived a giant in northern China named Kuafu. Not only was Kuafu tall and strong, he could also run at extraordinary speeds.

　　Kuafu went hunting in the mountains every day. One day, Kuafu saw a hare and threw a stone at it. The stone missed its target and the hare ran away. Kuafu started to give chase. He ran farther and farther, until darkness dawned. But he was still unable to catch up with the hare. Exhausted, Kuafu sat down on a rock to rest. He looked up and saw that the sun was about to set behind the mountain ranges

in the west. Kuafu thought, "If I catch hold of the sun and fix it in the sky, there will no longer be darkness in the world. How wonderful that will be!"

With that thought, he stood up and began to take big strides toward the direction where the sun was setting. Soon, he had run several thousand li and found himself at the Yu Valley. The Yu Valley was where the sun rested each day. Looking up, Kuafu saw a giant red fireball right above him. It was a gorgeous sight and Kuafu was overjoyed.

Suddenly, Kuafu felt an unbearable thirst. He bent over and drank from the Yellow River and the Wei River until the two rivers became dry. But that did not quench his burning thirst. He had no alternative but to run toward the north, for he knew that there was a large lake named Hanhai in the north and there was surely enough water there to quench his thirst. Unfortunately, the journey was too long for him. Kuafu died on the way because of thirst and exhaustion.

The giant, Kuafu, fell like a mountain. He took a last look at the setting sun, let out a long sigh, and with all his remaining strength, threw his wooden club forward before he stopped breathing.

When the sun rose again from the east and the bright light shone over the earth, people discovered that the giant who fell yesterday had gone missing. In his place there appeared a huge mountain with a peach forest at the foot of the mountain. The peaches were big and red. People associated the mountain

Five-Color Ponds

There was a legend that the celestial world had a Five-Color Pond, but in reality, there actually are numerous five-color ponds scattered throughout Canglong Mountain (Mountain of the Hidden Dragon) in the Sichuan Province. The larger ones cover an area of less than 1 mu (about 667 square meters) with water reaching a depth of less than 3 meters, and the smaller ones may be as big as a plate and contain water so shallow that one can easily feel the bottom of the pond. The golden border of the ponds surrounds it like a ribbon, taking on different shapes such as a bottle gourd, a sickle, or a fully bloomed lotus flower.

If one stands on top of the mountain and looks down, the ponds scattered all over the hillside appear to take on multiple colors such as red, yellow, green, and blue. What is puzzling is that although all the ponds are connected, the color of the water in each pond differs. In some ponds, the water in the upper region is coffee brown, yet when it flows to the lower region, it turns yellow. In other ponds, the water on the left may be blue, but when it flows to the right, it turns green. In yet other ponds, the water can take on many different colors but when one scoops some water out of it, the water is as crystal clear as ordinary water. This is so because there are many stalagmites at the bottom of the pond, and the surfaces of these stalagmites are covered with a thin layer of fine dust. Under the bright sunlight, the uneven bottoms of the pond act like reflective mirrors, reflecting different colors and hence creating the magical beauty of the five-color pond.

第八課

倉頡造字
jié

　　遠古的時候沒有文字，人們是靠結繩記事的。人們用各種不同顏色的繩子，表示各種不同的牲口、食物的數目。多一隻羊，打一個小結；多一頭牛，打一個大結。結滿十個就打成一個圈，十個圈就是一百。人們把繩子掛在牆上，賬目就全在那裏了。可是有時老鼠把繩子咬了，賬目就亂了。　再有，增加數目時，在繩子上打個結很方便；但是減少數目時，解開繩子上的結就麻煩了。

　　相傳倉頡是黃帝手下的官，他很聰明。黃帝讓他管牲口、食

物，他盡心盡力從不出錯。可是漸漸地，牲口和食物越來越多，事情也越來越多。光靠記憶和結繩已經不夠用了，怎麼才能不出錯呢？倉頡一直在想這個問題。

一天夜裏下了一場大雪。倉頡一早起來上山打獵，看見兩隻山雞在雪地上找食物。山雞走過，雪地上留下了兩行長長的爪印。接著，又有兩隻小鹿也跑出樹林，雪地上又留下了小鹿的蹄印。倉頡看得入了神。他想，把雞爪印畫出來就叫雞，把鹿蹄印畫出來就叫鹿。世界上任何東西，只要把它的形象畫出來不就成了字嗎？從這以後，倉頡把看到的山川、日月、鳥獸都創造成象形文字。不久，人、手、日、月、星、牛、羊、馬、雞、犬這些字都造出來了。

可是象形文字往哪裏寫呢？寫在木板上太笨重，寫在獸皮上也不合適。一天，有個人在河邊捉了一隻大龜，請倉頡給它造字。倉頡把龜細看了一遍，發現龜背上有排列整齊的方格子，便照龜的形象，造了個"龜"字，然後又把"龜"字刻在龜背上的方格子裏。龜由於背上刻字感到疼痛，乘人不防時，爬進河裏去了。三年以後，這隻背上刻字的龜，在另一個地方又被人捉住了。人們告訴倉頡，刻在龜背上的字不但沒有被水沖掉，而且還長大了，字跡也更明顯了……

從此以後，倉頡就讓人把捉到的龜的殼取下來，把造出的字都刻在龜殼上，然後用繩子串連起來，送給黃帝。黃帝看了很高興，讓人好好收藏。傳說從這時候起，中華民族就有了最早的象形文字。

生詞

cāng 倉	storehouse; Cang (surname)	xíng xiàng 形象	image; figure
shéng 繩	rope	chuàng zào 創造	create
biǎo shì 表示	indicate; show	hé shì 合適	suitable
shēng kou 牲口	livestock; beast of burden	pái liè 排列	put in order
yì quān 一圈	a circle	gé zi 格子	squares formed by crossed lines
zhàng mù 賬目	accounts	chéng 乘	take advantage of
jiǎnshǎo 減少	reduce	fáng 防	defend; protect
jì yì 記憶	memory	míngxiǎn 明顯	clear; distinct
tí yìn 蹄印	hoofprint	chuàn lián 串連	string together

聽寫

表示　牲口　一圈　賬目　減少　合適　排列

明顯　記憶　創造　串連　格子　*形象

比一比

增 { 增加 / 增多 }　　記 { 記憶 / 日記 }　　剩 { 剩下 / 剩飯 }

減 { 減少 / 減法 / 減肥 }　　結 { 結繩 / 結果 / 結婚 }　　乘 { 乘法 / 乘坐 / 乘車 }

反義詞

增加——減少　　　　笨重——輕便

麻煩——方便　　　　明顯——模糊

詞語解釋

牲口——人餵養的大動物，像牛、馬、羊、驢等。

明顯——很清楚。

表示——代表，說明。

形象——形狀，樣子。

趣味漢字（三）

種瓜得瓜

中國有一句古話："種瓜得瓜，種豆得豆。"中國人種瓜的歷史到底有多久了呢？科學家在中國遠古村落"河姆渡（mǔ dù）"的考古挖掘（jué）中，發現了公元前5,000年的冬瓜種子。這說明在中國人還沒有文字以前，冬瓜倒是種了很久了。種黃瓜、絲瓜等瓜類一般都要搭（dā）架子，瓜藤（téng）順著架子往上爬，瓜就挂在藤架上。我們在古代金文中看到的"瓜"字，就像藤上掛著一個瓜。

龜

我們看到的這個"龟"字是簡體字。它的繁（fán）體字為"龜"。再往前推，甲骨文中的龜字就是一個伸出頭尾和四隻腳的烏龜。

第八課

小知識

造字神——倉頡

倉頡是個傳說中的人物。有的說他是神，長著四隻眼睛，神光四射，發明了文字；也有的說他是黃帝的史官，所以他的家鄉叫史官鄉（在今陝西省白水縣）。他看見鳥獸在地上留下的爪蹄印，創造了中國的象形文字。

可以說，倉頡為整理中國古代文字做出了巨大貢(gòng)獻，他是許許多多文字創造者的化身。

陝西白水廟（倉頡廟）到今天還保存較(jiào)好。廟中有倉頡像和倉頡墓。

譯文 English Translation

Cangjie Creates Chinese Characters

In ancient China, there was no written word so people had to tie rope knots to record information. They used ropes of different colors to represent different kinds and amounts of livestock and food supplies. One small knot symbolized one lamb and one big knot signified one ox. Ten knots formed one circle and 10 circles stood for 100. People hung these ropes on the wall for accounts purposes. However, mice would occasionally bite a rope and break it, messing up the records. It was also easy to add by knotting, but difficult to record reductions in quantity as the knots had to be untied.

According to legend, Cangjie was an official of Huang Di. He was an extremely clever man. Huang Di assigned him to be in charge of livestock and food supplies. Cangjie was a hard worker who never made mistakes in his work. But as the amount of livestock and food supplies increased, more and more needed to be done. Simply relying on his memory and tying rope knots to keep records were no longer sufficient. He was constantly trying to think of other methods to record information accurately that wouldn't involve so much memory work.

One night it snowed very heavily. Early the next morning, Cangjie went hunting in the mountains when he saw two pheasants searching for food in the snow. Their footprints made a clear track in the snow. Then, two deer ran out of the forest, leaving their hoofprints in the snow. As Cangjie watched in amazement, he thought, "I can draw the footprints of a pheasant to represent pheasants, and the hoofprints of a deer to represent deer. If I can capture in a drawing the special characteristics that set apart each and every thing on the earth, that would be the perfect kind of character for writing!" From then on, Cangjie created pictographs for everything he saw, including the mountains, sun, moon, birds, and beasts. Soon, the characters of man, hand, sun, moon, star, ox, lamb, horse, chicken, and dog were all created.

But there arose another problem—where should these pictographs be written? Wood blocks were too heavy and inconvenient; animal skins were also not suitable. One day, a man caught a giant tortoise and brought it to Cangjie, asking him to create a character for it. Cangjie examined the tortoise carefully. He found neatly arranged squares on the tortoise's shell. He then created the character of tortoise (龜) and inscribed the word in one of the squares on the shell. Because of the pain from the inscription, the tortoise escaped and crawled back to the river when no one was watching. Three years later, the tortoise with the character inscribed on its back was caught again in another location. Cangjie was informed that instead of being washed away by the water, the character on the tortoise's back had become larger and clearer than before.

From then on, Cangjie ordered that tortoises that were caught should have their shells removed. He then inscribed the characters he created on the squares of the shell, strung them together, and presented them to Huang Di. Huang Di was delighted and ordered that the shells be stored carefully. This is the origin of Chinese pictographs according to legend.

Interesting Chinese Characters (III)

You Will Sow What You Reap

There is a traditional Chinese saying: Sow melons and you will reap melons, plant beans and you will harvest beans. How long has the Chinese been growing melons? During an excavation at the Hemudu Site in China, scientists found wax gourd seeds dating back to 5,000 B.C. This implies that the Chinese grew wax gourds long before they created Chinese characters. Treillage is needed for growing gourd plants such as the cucumber and towel gourd. Melon seedlings crawl upward along the treillage and fruits hang from it. This is why the character of melon (龜) in ancient times resembles a melon hanging from the treillage.

Tortoise

The character "龜" is simplified from the traditional character "龜" for tortoise. At the very beginning, this character in "jia gu wen" (inscriptions on bones or tortoise shells) was a picture of a tortoise with its head, tail, and four legs.

第九課

大禹治水

　　遠古的時候發了一場大水，連續二十二年。田地房屋全都淹沒了。有匹神馬叫"鯀（gǔn）"，他偷出了天帝的寶貝"息壤"來到人間。這息壤是一種長生不息的土壤，能把洪水吸乾。鯀因此得罪了天帝，被天帝殺死了。

　　鯀死後又發洪水。鯀的兒子禹決心繼承父業，治好洪水。禹

帶領人們疏通河道，引水下流。

一日，禹來到塗山，見到了山上部落首領的女兒女嬌，並和美麗的女嬌結了婚。婚後第四天，禹就離開女嬌出發去治水了。誰知這一去就是十三年。這十三年當中，禹三次經過自己的家門都沒有進去。

第一次是在他離家四年後。當禹走過家門口時，聽到母親的埋怨聲："父親治水，喪命在羽山；兒子治水，一去四年。"這時屋裏又傳出小孩的哭聲和女嬌長長的嘆氣聲。禹想：治水要緊。於是悄悄地離開了家。

二過家門是在他離家七年時。一聲長長的雞叫，傳得老遠老遠。屋裏傳出了他妻子和孩子的陣陣笑聲。禹想：這次，家裏是平平安安的，我就不進去了。於是，禹便繞過家門，向治水的工地奔去。

又過了三四年，禹第三次走過家門口，看見一個十來歲的男孩兒。那孩子對禹說："大伯，你認識禹嗎？他是我爹。他在治天下的洪水。請你給他帶個信，我奶奶和媽媽說叫他治好洪水再回家。"禹看見兒子，聽見他說話，心裏十分高興，說："我一定把口信帶到。"說完他就又轉身上馬走了。

三過家門而不入，就是這段故事。

第九課

　　禹為治水奮鬥了一生，華夏的山山水水，到處都留下了他的遺跡。其中最著名的是山西和陝西交界的龍門。那裏有兩座大山，立在黃河兩岸，形成了兩個天然的門扇。相傳，這兩扇門就是大禹治水時開鑿的。

　　大禹治水，給子孫萬代造福，人們感念他。禹後來繼承舜帝做了國君。他最後病死在浙江紹興。

生詞

yǔ 禹	Yu (name)	diē 爹	father
lián xù 連續	continuously	yí dìng 一定	certainly; surely
tǔ rǎng 土壤	soil	fèn dòu 奮鬥	strive
hóngshuǐ 洪水	flood	huá xià 華夏	archaic name for China
xī 吸	absorb	yí jì 遺跡	historical remains
jì chéng 繼承	carry on; succeed to	kāi záo 開鑿	excavate; cut
shū tōng 疏通	dredge; remove obstacles form	shùn 舜	Shun (name)
mán yuàn 埋怨	complain		

聽寫

禹　土壤　連續　洪水　遺跡　奮鬥　埋怨

繼承　爹　華夏　*開鑿

比一比

承 { 承認 / 繼承 }　續 { 連續 / 繼續 }　奮 { 發奮 / 奮鬥 }　遺 { 遺跡 / 遺產 }

詞語運用

連續　繼續

這些天連續下雨，路上都是水。

白天姐姐沒有做完作業，晚上只好繼續做。

帶領　衣領

大禹帶領人們治水十三年。

這件衣服的衣領太髒了。

同音字

段　斷

每天晚上，媽媽都給小晨晨講一段故事。

大風把電線颳斷了。

多音字

mái
埋
mái
埋入

mán
埋
mán
埋怨

閱讀

黃河上的"龍門"

中國有一個"鯉(lǐ)魚跳龍門"的故事，是說大海裏的魚兒從黃河口游向黃河上游。魚兒們一路逆(nì)水，游得十分辛苦，游到龍門的時候已經完全沒有力氣了。龍門兩岸是高山，中間夾著黃河，河水從高處向下奔流，勢不可擋。魚兒們要拼命往上游，往上跳。魚兒要是能跳過龍門就能到達上游變成龍；跳

不過去就永遠是魚。對魚兒來說，龍門是最後一關，也是最重要的一關。可這個龍門到底在哪兒呢？

傳說禹的父親鯀治水九年，沒有成功，被舜殺了。舜看到洪水淹沒了田野，沖走了糧食、牲口，人們生活十分困苦，心中難受，又派禹去治水。

禹並沒有記恨舜，而是一心治水。他看到父親用土和石頭攔(lán)水的辦法不行，就採用疏通河道，引水流入大海的辦法治水。

在治黃河時，禹從青海黃河上游，一段一段沿河看水情，通河道。當黃河流到山西時，被一座大山——龍門山擋住了去路。河水流不出去就成了洪水。一定要鑿開龍門山，把黃河水引入大海。可是要鑿開龍門山，比上天還難哪！禹帶領大家用石頭工具來開山。一連幹了好幾年，不分春夏秋冬，颳風下雨，禹帶著大家鑿山不止，終于鑿開了龍門山。當黃河水通過龍門山奔騰(téng)向東流去時，禹和治水大軍都歡呼起來。禹治水成功了！這個在龍門山鑿開的口子叫禹門，也就是傳說中"鯉魚跳龍門"的龍門。

Yu the Great Subdues the Flood

A long time ago, there was a terrible flood that lasted 22 years. Cropland and houses were all washed away. A celestial horse named Gun stole the Celestial Ruler's precious "xi rang", a piece of magic soil which could dry up the floodwaters, and came to the mortal world. The Celestial Ruler was very angry and Gun was executed.

After Gun died, the torrential flood raged again. Yu, Gun's son, determined to follow his father's example to control the flood. He led his men to dig channels to divert the floodwaters and these channels served as outlets for the water into the sea.

One day, Yu came to the Tu Mountain. He met and married Nvjiao, the beautiful daughter of the tribal chief. Four days after the wedding ceremony, Yu left his wife to tame the raging waters. During the next 13 years, despite passing his own house three times, he never once stopped in for a visit.

The first time Yu passed his house was four years after he had left home. As he walked past the gate, he heard his mother complain, "The father went to contain the floodwaters and died at the Yu Mountain. The son left to control the flood and has not returned in four years." He heard the cries of a baby and the sighs of his wife. Concluding that controlling the flood was more crucial, Yu left quietly.

The second time Yu passed his house was seven years after he had left home. The rooster was crowing, and his wife and child were laughing. Yu thought, "Since everyone is well, I shall not enter." So he walked past his house and rushed to continue his task of taming the flood.

After another three to four years, Yu passed his own house a third time. This time, he saw a teenage boy. The boy said to Yu, "Uncle, do you know Yu? He is my father and is now working hard to control the flood. If you meet him, please give him this message: my grandmother and mother want him to tame the flood before coming back home." Yu knew this was his son and his words pleased him. He said to his son, "I will give him your message." He then mounted his horse and left.

This is the story of Yu passing his own house three times and not entering.

Yu devoted his entire life to taming the flood and left many traces in all parts of China, among which the most famous is the Longmen (Dragon Gate) located at the border of Shanxi and Shaanxi Province. The two mountains standing at the two sides of the Yellow River create a natural gate. According to legend, the gate was created by Yu to channel the floodwaters.

People remember, and are grateful to, Yu the Great for controlling the flood and bringing prosperity to many generations. He later succeeded Shun and ruled the country. Yu died of illness in Shaoxing, Zhejiang Province.

 中國神話傳說

The Dragon Gate along the Yellow River

There is a story in China about carps that jump over the Dragon Gate. This story tells of how fishes from the sea swim upstream from the mouth of the Yellow River. By the time the fishes reach the Dragon Gate, they are all tired out because they have to swim against the current. Both banks of the Dragon Gate were flanked by high mountains and it is at this area where the water flows downward with a great force. The fishes have to try their best to swim and jump over the Gate against the strong current. It is believed that only those fishes that succeed in jumping over the Dragon Gate can reach the upstream area and transform into dragons; those that fail remain as fishes forever. Hence, the Dragon Gate is the last and the most important barrier for the fishes to overcome. But where can the Dragon Gate be found?

According to legend, Gun, Yu's father, spent nine years trying in vain to control the flood and was then killed by Shun for his failure. Seeing how the flood destroyed cropland, livestock, and food supplies, and how the people suffered, Shun felt sorry for them and sent Yu to tame the flood.

Yu did not blame Shun for killing his father; instead, he devoted himself to the task assigned him. Yu saw that his father's method of attempting to stop the floodwaters with earth and rocks was not effective and thus he adopted another method by digging channels and diverting the water into the sea.

In order to tame the Yellow River, Yu made a careful survey of the river, section by section, digging ditches along each section. When the Yellow River flowed to the Shanxi Province, the Longmen (Dragon Gate) Mountain blocked the river flow and this caused turbulent waters which overflowed the banks resulting in floods. Yu determined to cut a channel through the mountain and to make it possible for water to flow by way of this channel. Although it was a formidable task, Yu worked with his men regardless of rain or shine, digging and cutting through the mountain, through all the four seasons in a year. After many years of continuous effort, they succeeded. When the Yellow River rushed through the Longmen Mountain eastward to the sea, Yu and his men cheered loudly. The opening they cut in the Longmen Mountain was named Yumen (Yu Gate), and this is the Dragon Gate the legendary carps jumped over.

生字表（繁）

1. 暗(àn) 宇(yǔ) 宙(zhòu) 斧(fǔ) 巨(jù) 濁(zhuó) 疲(pí) 呼(hū) 液(yè) 肌(jī) 筋(jīn) 輝(huī) 潔(jié) 膚(fū) 礦(kuàng) 闢(pì)

2. 媧(wā) 辰(chén) 翠(cuì) 鳴(míng) 昏(hūn) 孤(gū) 潑(pō) 揑(niē) 差(chà) 休(xiū) 笨(bèn) 柔(róu) 婚(hūn)

3. 輪(lún) 枯(kū) 嫦(cháng) 娥(é) 唬(hu) 搗(dǎo) 剩(shèng) 返(fǎn) 凡(fán)

4. 決(jué) 希(xī) 怨(yuàn) 恨(hèn) 罰(fá) 漸(jiàn) 棄(qì) 悔(huǐ) 念(niàn)

5. 嚐(cháng) 肝(gān) 挨(ái) 糧(liáng) 暈(yūn) 吐(tù) 證(zhèng) 嘗(cháng) 腸(cháng) 寸(cùn) 竟(jìng) 獻(xiàn) 鼎(dǐng)

6. 料(liào) 哀(āi) 撕(sī) 裂(liè) 肯(kěn) 嬌(jiāo) 至(zhì) 濤(tāo) 洶(xiōng) 涌(yǒng) 願(yuàn) 勿(wù) 吾(wú) 榮(róng) 填(tián) 依(yī) 投(tóu) 誓(shì)

7. 歪(wāi) 固(gù) 邁(mài) 煌(huáng) 伏(fú) 途(tú) 遙(yáo) 似(shì) 杖(zhàng) 拋(pāo) 吸(xī) 尋(xún)

8. 倉(cāng) 繩(shéng) 牲(shēng) 圈(quān) 賬(zhàng) 減(jiǎn) 憶(yì) 蹄(tí) 創(chuàng) 適(shì) 列(liè) 格(gé) 乘(chéng) 防(fáng) 串(chuàn)

9. 禹(yǔ) 續(xù) 壤(rǎng) 洪(hóng) 繼(jì) 疏(shū) 爹(diē) 奮(fèn) 遺(yí) 鑿(záo) 舜(shùn)

共計116個生字

生字表（简）

1. 暗(àn) 宇(yǔ) 宙(zhòu) 斧(fǔ) 巨(jù) 浊(zhuó) 疲(pí) 呼(hū) 液(yè) 肌(jī) 筋(jīn) 辉(huī) 洁(jié) 肤(fū) 矿(kuàng) 辟(pì)

2. 娲(wā) 辰(chén) 翠(cuì) 鸣(míng) 昏(hūn) 孤(gū) 泼(pō) 捏(niē) 差(chà) 休(xiū) 笨(bèn) 柔(róu) 婚(hūn)

3. 轮(lún) 枯(kū) 嫦(cháng) 娥(é) 唬(hu) 捣(dǎo) 剩(shèng) 返(fǎn) 凡(fán)

4. 决(jué) 希(xī) 怨(yuàn) 恨(hèn) 罚(fá) 渐(jiàn) 弃(qì) 悔(huǐ) 念(niàn)

5. 尝(cháng) 肝(gān) 挨(ái) 粮(liáng) 晕(yūn) 吐(tù) 证(zhèng) 肠(cháng) 寸(cùn) 竟(jìng) 献(xiàn) 鼎(dǐng)

6. 料(liào) 哀(āi) 撕(sī) 裂(liè) 肯(kěn) 娇(jiāo) 至(zhì) 涛(tāo) 汹(xiōng) 涌(yǒng) 愿(yuàn) 勿(wù) 吾(wú) 荣(róng) 填(tián) 依(yī) 投(tóu) 誓(shì)

7. 歪(wāi) 固(gù) 迈(mài) 煌(huáng) 伏(fú) 途(tú) 遥(yáo) 似(shì) 杖(zhàng) 抛(pāo) 吸(xī) 寻(xún)

8. 仓(cāng) 绳(shéng) 牲(shēng) 圈(quān) 账(zhàng) 减(jiǎn) 忆(yì) 蹄(tí) 创(chuàng) 适(shì) 列(liè) 格(gé) 乘(chéng) 防(fáng) 串(chuàn)

9. 禹(yǔ) 续(xù) 壤(rǎng) 洪(hóng) 继(jì) 疏(shū) 爹(diē) 奋(fèn) 遗(yí) 凿(záo) 舜(shùn)

共计115个生字

生詞表（繁）

1. 黑暗(hēi àn) 宇宙(yǔ zhòu) 斧頭(fǔ tou) 巨大(jù dà) 濁(zhuó) 一丈(yí zhàng) 鬆口氣(sōng kǒu qì) 疲勞(pí láo) 呼出(hū chū) 血液(xuè yè) 肌肉(jī ròu) 筋脈(jīn mài) 四通八達(sì tōng bā dá) 光輝(guāng huī) 潔白(jié bái) 皮膚(pí fū) 礦物(kuàng wù) 開天闢地(kāi tiān pì dì) 裝點(zhuāng diǎn)

2. 女媧(nǚ wā) 星辰(xīng chén) 翠(cuì) 鳴(míng) 黃昏(huáng hūn) 孤獨(gū dú) 活潑(huó pō) 生命(shēng mìng) 倒影(dào yǐng) 捏(niē) 差不多(chà bu duō) 居然(jū rán) 趕緊(gǎn jǐn) 休息(xiū xi) 笨(bèn) 陽剛(yáng gāng) 陰柔(yīn róu) 人類(rén lèi) 結婚(jié hūn) 生兒育女(shēng ér yù nǚ) 安寧(ān níng)

3. 輪流(lún liú) 曬枯(shài kū) 難受(nán shòu) 胡鬧(hú nào) 嫦娥(cháng é) 嚇唬(xià hu) 搗亂(dǎo luàn) 剩下(shèng xià) 涼快(liáng kuai) 歡呼(huān hū) 驚慌(jīng huāng) 要求(yāo qiú) 返回(fǎn huí) 英雄(yīng xióng) 悶悶不樂(mèn mèn bú lè) 凡人(fán rén)

4. 決定(jué dìng) 同情(tóng qíng) 希望(xī wàng) 怨恨(yuàn hèn) 自作自受(zì zuò zì shòu) 罰(fá) 漸漸(jiàn jiàn) 背棄(bèi qì) 失望(shī wàng) 冷清(lěng qīng) 桂花(guì huā) 後悔(hòu huǐ) 思念(sī niàn)

5. 嚐(cháng) 炎帝(yán dì) 透明(tòu míng) 心肝(xīn gān) 五臟(wǔ zàng) 挨餓(ái è) 五穀雜糧(wǔ gǔ zá liáng) 頭暈(tóu yūn) 吐(tù) 證明(zhèng míng) 嘗試(cháng shì) 解毒(jiě dú) 所有(suǒ yǒu) 解救(jiě jiù) 藥方(yào fāng) 不幸(bú xìng) 腸子(cháng zi) 寸(cùn) 竟然(jìng rán) 獻出(xiàn chū) 世代(shì dài) 懷念(huái niàn) 鼎(dǐng)

6. 填 不料 悲痛 悲哀 撕裂 取名 不肯 嬌女 至
波濤洶涌 勿 吾 以……為榮 蒼翠 依然 但願
讚美 決心 一刻不停 投 發誓

7. 歪 固定 邁開 輝煌 伏下 足夠 路途 遙遠 中途
像……似的 木杖 拋 呼吸 照耀 尋求

8. 倉頡 繩 表示 牲口 一圈 賬目 減少 記憶 蹄印
形象 創造 合適 排列 格子 乘 防 明顯 串連

9. 大禹 連續 土壤 洪水 吸 繼承 疏通 埋怨 爹 一定
奮鬥 華夏 遺跡 開鑿 舜

共計162個生詞

生词表（简）

1. 黑暗 hēi àn　宇宙 yǔ zhòu　斧头 fǔ tou　巨大 jù dà　浊 zhuó　一丈 yí zhàng　松口气 sōngkǒu qì　疲劳 pí láo　呼出 hū chū　血液 xuè yè　肌肉 jī ròu　筋脉 jīn mài　四通八达 sì tōng bā dá　光辉 guāng huī　洁白 jié bái　皮肤 pí fū　矿物 kuàng wù　开天辟地 kāi tiān pì dì　装点 zhuāngdiǎn

2. 女娲 nǚ wā　星辰 xīngchén　翠鸣 cuì míng　黄昏 huánghūn　孤独 gū dú　活泼 huó pō　生命 shēngmìng　倒影 dàoyǐng　捏 niē　差不多 chà bu duō　居然 jū rán　赶紧 gǎn jǐn　休息 xiū xi　笨 bèn　阳刚 yánggāng　阴柔 yīn róu　人类 rén lèi　结婚 jié hūn　生儿育女 shēng ér yù nǚ　安宁 ān níng

3. 轮流 lún liú　晒枯 shài kū　难受 nánshòu　胡闹 hú nào　嫦娥 cháng é　吓唬 xià hu　捣乱 dǎoluàn　剩下 shèng xià　凉快 liángkuai　欢呼 huān hū　惊慌 jīnghuāng　要求 yāo qiú　返回 fǎn huí　英雄 yīngxióng　闷闷不乐 mènmèn bú lè　凡人 fán rén

4. 决定 jué dìng　同情 tóngqíng　希望 xī wàng　怨恨 yuànhèn　自作自受 zì zuò zì shòu　罚 fá　渐渐 jiànjiàn　背弃 bèi qì　失望 shī wàng　冷清 lěngqing　桂花 guì huā　后悔 hòu huǐ　思念 sī niàn

5. 尝 cháng　炎帝 yán dì　透明 tòu míng　心肝 xīn gān　五脏 wǔ zàng　挨饿 ái è　五谷杂粮 wǔ gǔ zá liáng　头晕 tóu yūn　吐 tù　证明 zhèngmíng　尝试 cháng shì　解毒 jiě dú　所有 suǒyǒu　解救 jiě jiù　药方 yàofāng　不幸 bú xìng　肠子 cháng zi　寸 cùn　竟然 jìng rán　献出 xiànchū　世代 shì dài　怀念 huáinián　鼎 dǐng

6. 填 不料 悲痛 悲哀 撕裂 取名 不肯 娇女 至
   波涛 汹涌 勿 吾 以……为荣 苍翠 依然 但愿
   赞美 决心 一刻不停 投 发誓

7. 歪 固定 迈开 辉煌 伏下 足够 路途 遥远 中途
   像……似的 木杖 抛 呼吸 照耀 寻求

8. 仓颉 绳 表示 牲口 一圈 账目 减少 记忆 蹄印
   形象 创造 合适 排列 格子 乘 防 明显 串连

9. 大禹 连续 土壤 吸 洪水 继承 疏通 埋怨 爹 一定
   奋斗 华夏 遗迹 开凿 舜

共计162个生词

《雙雙中文教材》是一套專門為海外學生編寫的中文教材。它是由美國加州王雙雙老師和中國專家學者共同努力，在海外多年的實踐中編寫出來的。全書共20冊，識字量2500個，包括了從識字、拼音、句型、短文的學習，到初步的較系統的中國文化的學習。教材大體介紹了中國地理、歷史、哲學等方面的豐富內容，突出了中國文化的魅力。課本知識面廣，趣味性強，深入淺出，易教易學。

　　這套教材體系完整、構架靈活、使用面廣。學生可以從零起點開始，一直學完全部課程20冊；也可以將後11冊（10～20冊）的九個文化專題和第五冊（漢語拼音）單獨使用，這樣便於開設中國哲學、地理、歷史等專門課程以及假期班、短期中國文化班、拼音速成班的高中和大學使用，符合了美國AP中文課程的目標和基本要求。

　　本書是《雙雙中文教材》的第十三冊，適用於已學習掌握800個以上漢字的學生使用。中國神話傳說多產生於遠古的黃河流域，那時還沒有文字。中華民族的祖先在與自然搏鬥、求得生存的過程中戰勝了乾旱、洪水、疾病等重重困難，生存下來、發展起來，並創造了綿延至今的中華文明。本冊介紹了10篇美麗的神話傳說。學生們在進入這個神話世界時，會看到遠古時期中華民族的祖先與自然搏鬥時激動人心的場面，體會到中華民族勤勞勇敢、聰明智慧這些優良傳統源遠流長。

ISBN 978-7-301-14205-9

定價：90.00元

含課本、練習冊和CD-ROM一張

第一課

一　寫生詞

黑	暗										
宇	宙										
斧	頭										
巨	大										
濁											
疲	勞										
呼	出										
血	液										
肌	肉										
筋	脈										
光	輝										
潔	白										
皮	膚										

礦	物									

開	天	闢	地							

二 組詞

暗_____ 音_____ 宇_____ 睜_____

圍_____ 斧_____ 巨_____ 輝_____

疲_____ 礦_____ 汗_____ 肌_____

良_____ 脈_____ 潔_____ 呼_____

膚_____ 闢_____ 液_____ 富_____

三 把正確的字連線組詞

液　　　　　　暗　　　　　　彩
血　　　　黑　　　　雲
　　夜　　　　　　音　　　　　　踩

　　虎　　　　　　巨　　　　　　劈
皮　　　　大　　　　開
　　膚　　　　　　臣　　　　　　闢

四 在括號中寫上合適的形容詞

（　　　）的太陽　（　　　）的月亮　（　　　）的星星

五　造句

   1. 周圍 _____

   2. 四通八達 _____

六　根據課文判斷對錯

   1. 盤古用大刀闢開天地。　　　　　　　___對　___錯

   2. 盤古怕天地合起來，就用頭頂著天，腳踩著地。　　　　　　　　　　　　　___對　___錯

   3. 盤古是累死的。　　　　　　　　　　___對　___錯

   4. 盤古的血液變成了江河湖海。　　　　___對　___錯

   5. 盤古的右眼變成了太陽，左眼變成了月亮。　　　　　　　　　　　　　　　___對　___錯

   6. 盤古開天闢地，又用自己的身體裝點世界。　　　　　　　　　　　　　　　___對　___錯

七 選詞填空

> 疲勞　　鬍子　　盤子　　一頂　　皮膚

1. _____裏裝滿了水果。

2. 他長著長長的_____。

3. 他太_____了,剛一躺下就睡著了。

4. 朋友送我_____黃色的草帽。

5. 小妹妹老在太陽下面玩兒,把_____都曬黑了。

八 根據閱讀材料《中國的姓氏(shì)》回答問題

1. 什麼字是由"女"和"生"組成的?

答:_____

2. 華人最大的三個姓是什麼?_____

3. 中國有本古書專門收集中國人的姓氏,叫_____

4. 在中國山東省,姓什麼的人比較多?_____

5. 在中國廣東省,姓什麼的人比較多?_____

6. 在中國四川省,姓什麼的人比較多?_____

7. 你們班上有多少同學？他們姓什麼？請寫出六個以上的姓氏。

_____

_____

九　縮寫課文《盤古開天地》（最少寫六句話）

_____

_____

_____

_____

_____

十　朗讀課文三遍

第三課

一　寫生詞

輪	流										
曬	枯										
嫦	娥										
嚇	唬										
搗	亂										
剩	下										
返	回										
凡	人										

二　組詞

傳＿＿＿　　輪＿＿＿　　總＿＿＿　　剩＿＿＿

曬＿＿＿　　喘＿＿＿　　鬧＿＿＿　　訓＿＿＿

返＿＿＿　　妻＿＿＿　　故＿＿＿　　嚇＿＿＿

難_____ 雄_____ 搗_____ 歡_____

要_____ 既_____ 遲_____ 驚_____

三 比一比，再組詞

驚_____ 搗_____ 氣_____ 剩_____
馬_____ 島_____ 汽_____ 乘_____

英_____ 唬_____ 輪_____ 求_____
應_____ 虎_____ 論_____ 救_____

四 寫出反義詞

炎熱——　　　　　快快樂樂——

五 選詞填空

> 帽子　眼睛　牛　魚　草地
> 大雨　花狗　竹子　巨響

一條（　　）　　一片（　　）　　一雙（　　）

一群（　　）　　一隻（　　）　　一根（　　）

一聲（　　）　　一陣（　　）　　一頂（　　）

六 造句

　　1. 更＿＿＿＿＿＿＿＿＿＿＿＿＿＿＿＿＿＿＿＿＿＿

　　2. 難受＿＿＿＿＿＿＿＿＿＿＿＿＿＿＿＿＿＿＿＿＿

　　3. 熱鬧＿＿＿＿＿＿＿＿＿＿＿＿＿＿＿＿＿＿＿＿＿

七 根據課文判斷對錯

　　1. 很久以前，天上忽然出現了八個太陽。　　＿＿對　＿＿錯

　　2. 天帝叫羿帶著嫦娥到人間去玩一玩。　　＿＿對　＿＿錯

　　3. 羿把天空中的太陽全部射下來了。　　＿＿對　＿＿錯

　　4. 天帝的兒子是金黃色的三足烏鴉。　　＿＿對　＿＿錯

　　5. 天帝看見羿返回天上，心裏十分高興。　　＿＿對　＿＿錯

　　6. 凡人是不會死的。　　＿＿對　＿＿錯

八 根據閱讀材料《神射手──羿》選詞填空

　　　　樹林　　咬住　　眼睛

　　1. 一次，突然從＿＿＿＿＿裏射出一支箭。

　　2. 羿張開嘴＿＿＿＿＿箭頭。

3. 羿讓徒弟做兩件事情：一要學會不眨^{zhǎ}_____，二要學會把小東西看成大東西。

九　縮寫課文《羿射九日》（最少寫六句話）

_____
_____
_____
_____
_____

十　朗讀課文三遍

第五課

一 寫生詞

嚐											
心	肝										
挨	餓										
五	穀	雜	糧								
頭	暈										
吐											
證	明										
腸	子										
寸											
竟	然										
獻	出										
鼎											

二 組詞

善_____　　透_____　　禾_____　　腸_____

暈_____　　痛_____　　嚐_____　　毒_____

救_____　　證_____　　獻_____　　懷_____

藥_____　　世_____　　命_____　　肝_____

糧_____　　緊_____　　暈_____　　竟_____

三 寫出反義詞

出——　　　遠——　　　來——

後——　　　生——　　　新——

輕——　　　遲——

四 選詞填空

> 炎熱　透氣　解開　常常　長長　嚐嚐

1. 門窗關著,房子一點也不_____。

2. 北京的夏天,天氣十分_____。

3. 奶奶病了,我幫她_____衣服,讓她躺下。

4. 雖然學校離家很遠,但是姐姐_____走回家。

5. 我們走進一家日本飯館，想_____日本菜。

6. 她有大大的眼睛和_____的頭髮。

五 造句

例句：他不但作文好，還能寫詩歌。

爸爸離開家鄉時間太長了，孩子們竟然不認識他。

1. 不但……還_____

2. 竟然_____

六 根據課文判斷對錯

1. 炎帝就是太陽神。　　　　　　　　　　___對　___錯

2. 炎帝教人們種五穀，可人們還是沒吃沒穿。___對　___錯

3. 神農為了給人們治病，決心自己嚐百草。___對　___錯

4. 神農的身子是透明的。　　　　　　　　___對　___錯

5. 神農救了許多人。　　　　　　　　　　___對　___錯

6. 神農是被毒蛇咬死的。　　　　　　　　___對　___錯

7. 人們世世代代懷念神農。　　　　　　　___對　___錯

七 根據閱讀材料《針灸(jiǔ)的起源》回答問題

    1. 針灸在中國有多少年的歷史了？

    答：_____

    2. 針灸包括哪兩種古老的治病辦法？這兩種辦法是怎麼治病的？（不少於三句話）

    答：_____

    _____

    _____

八 縮寫課文《神農嚐百草》（最少寫六句話）

_____

_____

_____

_____

_____

_____

九 朗讀課文三遍

第七課

一 寫生詞

歪											
固	定										
邁	開										
輝	煌										
伏	下										
路	途										
遙	遠										
像	…	…	似	的							
木	杖										
拋											
呼	吸										
尋	求										

二　組詞

遙_____　　邁_____　　善_____　　輝_____

固_____　　夠_____　　尋_____　　杖_____

勇_____　　拋_____　　煌_____　　伏_____

途_____　　似_____　　耀_____

三　選字填空

1. 我們去爬山，爬到山頂時，出了一身大_____（汗　漢）

2. 夸父_____開大步跑起來。（邁　萬）

3. 這個紅書包比那個藍書包_____貴。（更　便）

4. 下課了，同學們跑出教室去_____息。（休　木）

5. 我家門前有一_____大山。（坐　座）

6. 國王和他的衛_____很快地上了船。（士　土）

四　造句

1. 像……似的_____

2. 一會兒_____

五　根據課文判斷對錯

1. 夸父力大無窮。　　　　　　　　　　　　　　___對　___錯

2. 夸父想要捉住太陽，固定在天空，讓大地永遠是一片光明。　　　　　　　　　　　　　___對　___錯

3. 夸父一口氣把黃河和渭(wèi)河的水都喝乾了。　___對　___錯

4. 夸父的身體化成山，夸父的手杖變成桃林。　___對　___錯

5. 一顆顆鮮桃是夸父留給猴子的。　　　　　　___對　___錯

六　相配詞連線

路途　　　　木杖

邁開　　　　大地

停止　　　　遙遠

拋出　　　　大步

照耀　　　　呼吸

七 根據閱讀材料《五彩池》判斷對錯

　　1. 五彩池位於崑崙山。　　　　　　　　＿＿對　＿＿錯

　　2. 滿山坡的五彩池多得數不清。　　　　＿＿對　＿＿錯

　　3. 五彩池的形狀各種各樣。　　　　　　＿＿對　＿＿錯

　　4. 每個池中的水顏色不同是形成五彩池的

　　　　原因。　　　　　　　　　　　　　＿＿對　＿＿錯

八 縮寫課文《夸父追日》（最少寫六句話）

_____

_____

_____

_____

_____

九 朗讀課文三遍

第九課

一 寫生詞

禹											
連	續										
土	壤										
洪	水										
繼	承										
疏	通										
爹											
奮	鬥										
遺	跡										
開	鑿										
舜											

二　組詞

繼_____　　淹_____　　寶_____　　領_____

壞_____　　疏_____　　婚_____　　喪_____

繞_____　　遺_____　　福_____　　埋_____

續_____　　洪_____　　處_____　　緊_____

三　比一比，再組詞

{ 直_____　　{ 低_____　　{ 住_____
  真_____ 　　 底_____　　 往_____

{ 洪_____　　{ 後_____　　{ 新_____
  紅_____　　 候_____　　 欣_____

四　選詞填空

> 就　於是　奔　奮鬥　向　繞過

1. 大禹為治水_____了一生。

2. 大禹_____家門，_____治水的工地_____去。

3. 家裏是平平安安的，我_____不進去了。

4. 大禹想治水要緊，_____悄悄地離開了家。

五 造句

　　1. 一定＿＿＿＿＿＿＿＿＿＿＿＿＿＿＿＿＿＿＿

　　2. 到處＿＿＿＿＿＿＿＿＿＿＿＿＿＿＿＿＿＿＿

六 根據課文判斷對錯

　　1. 大禹的兒子名字叫鯀(gǔn)。　　＿＿對　＿＿錯

　　2. 大禹和美麗的女嬌結了婚。　　＿＿對　＿＿錯

　　3. 大禹治水十三年，三過家門而不入。　＿＿對　＿＿錯

　　4. 相傳，龍門就是大禹治水時開鑿的。　＿＿對　＿＿錯

　　5. 大禹後來繼承舜帝做了國君。　　＿＿對　＿＿錯

　　6. 大禹最後病死在浙江紹(shào)興。　＿＿對　＿＿錯

七 根據閱讀材料《黃河上的"龍門"》選詞填空

> 要是　永遠　龍門　上游
> 奔流　黃河口　大海　疲勞

　　中國有一個"鯉魚跳（　　）"的故事，是説（　　）裏的魚兒從（　　）游向黃河的（　　）。魚兒們游到龍門的時候，已

經很（　　）了。黃河從龍門的高處向下（　　），勢不可擋。魚兒們要拼命往上游，往上跳。魚兒（　　）能跳過龍門就能到達上游變成龍，跳不過去就（　　）是魚。

八　縮寫《大禹治水》"三過家門而不入"這段故事（最少寫六句話）

九　朗讀課文三遍

第一課聽寫

第三課聽寫

第五課聽寫

第七課聽寫

第九課聽寫

王雙雙 編著
Shuangshuang Wang

雙雙中文教材（13）
Chinese Language and Culture Course

練 習 册
（第十三册　雙課）

姓名：＿＿＿＿＿＿＿＿

年級：＿＿＿＿＿＿＿＿

第二課

一　寫生詞

女	媧										
星	辰										
翠											
鳴											
黃	昏										
孤	獨										
活	潑										
捏											
差	不	多									
休	息										
笨											
陰	柔										
結	婚										

1

二　組詞

昏＿＿＿＿　　娲＿＿＿＿　　孤＿＿＿＿　　潑＿＿＿＿

命＿＿＿＿　　影＿＿＿＿　　辰＿＿＿＿　　緊＿＿＿＿

圍＿＿＿＿　　娃＿＿＿＿　　育＿＿＿＿　　柔＿＿＿＿

類＿＿＿＿　　休＿＿＿＿　　居＿＿＿＿　　差＿＿＿＿

三　選字組詞

遲（到　倒）　　　摸一（模　摸）　　　模（樣　洋）

四　把正確的字連線組詞

到　　　　　　常　　　　　　在

昏　　　　非　　　　現

倒　　　　　　長　　　　　　再

五　在括號中寫上合適的形容詞

（　　　）的河水　（　　　）的倒影　（　　　）的小娃娃

（　　　）的生命　（　　　）的日子　（　　　）的女娲

六 造句

    1. 突然 _____

    2. 趕緊 _____

七 根據課文判斷對錯

    1. 女媧一個人在世界上感到非常快樂。   ___對   ___錯

    2. 她看見河水中自己美麗的倒影，就有了

       造人的想法。   ___對   ___錯

    3. 最早的人是女媧捏成的。   ___對   ___錯

    4. 男人身上被吹了陰柔之氣。   ___對   ___錯

    5. 女人身上被吹了陽剛之氣。   ___對   ___錯

    6. 為了讓人類一代代傳下去，女媧讓男人

       恨女人。   ___對   ___錯

    7. 人們日出而息，日落而作，過著和平安寧

       的日子。   ___對   ___錯

中國神話傳說

八 縮寫閱讀材料《女媧補天》(線索：時間、地點、發生了什麼)

1. 故事發生在什麼時候？

2. 天為什麼倒了？

3. 哪座山倒了？

4. 女媧心裏怎麼想的？她做了些什麼？

5. 為什麼河水向東流？

_____

_____

_____

_____

_____

_____

_____

九 朗讀課文三遍

第四課

一 寫生詞

決	定										
希	望										
怨	恨										
罰											
漸	漸										
背	棄										
后	悔										
思	念										

二 組詞

崙_____　　　神_____　　　奔_____　　　決_____

漸_____　　　離_____　　　情_____　　　棄_____

怨_____　　　念_____　　　希_____　　　悔_____

永_____　　　眾_____　　　怕_____　　　罰_____

望＿＿＿　　悄＿＿＿　　桂＿＿＿　　冷＿＿＿

返＿＿＿　　自＿＿＿　　受＿＿＿

三　先用原字組詞，再加偏旁組成新字，並用新字組詞

令＿＿＿　　　　每＿＿＿　　　　田＿＿＿

（冷）＿＿＿　　（　）＿＿＿　　（　）＿＿＿

果＿＿＿　　　　青＿＿＿　　　　門＿＿＿

（　）＿＿＿　　（　）＿＿＿　　（　）＿＿＿

四　讀一讀，注意"的、地、得"的使用

1. 羿高高興興地回到家裏。

2. 她只能永遠生活在冷冷清清的月宮裏。

3. 人們熱得喘不上氣來。

4. 嫦娥的腳漸漸地離開了地面。

5. 人們過著和平安寧的日子。

五　造句

例句:小華游泳比賽沒得第一,她感到很失望。

弟弟希望我跟他一起玩兒。

嫦娥決定獨自一個人回天上去。

1. 失望＿＿＿＿＿＿＿＿＿＿＿＿＿＿＿＿＿＿＿

2. 希望＿＿＿＿＿＿＿＿＿＿＿＿＿＿＿＿＿＿＿

3. 決定＿＿＿＿＿＿＿＿＿＿＿＿＿＿＿＿＿＿＿

六　填空

月宮非常＿＿＿＿,讓嫦娥很失望。她想返回＿＿＿＿,可是已經不行了。想起丈夫的好處,她很＿＿＿＿。她只能永遠留在月宮裏＿＿＿＿她的丈夫。

七　根據課文判斷對錯

1. 崑崙山上的東王母有長生不老藥。　　　＿＿對　＿＿錯

2. 羿感到人間也不錯。　　　　　　　　　＿＿對　＿＿錯

3. 羿準備和嫦娥一同吃不死藥。　　　　　＿＿對　＿＿錯

4. 嫦娥只想著自己,並不關心羿。　　　　＿＿對　＿＿錯

5. 嫦娥背棄了她的丈夫。　　　　　___對　___錯

6. 月宮裏只有一隻玉兔和一棵桂花樹。　___對　___錯

7. 嫦娥在月宮裏並不快樂。　　　　　___對　___錯

八　根據閱讀材料《中秋節》判斷對錯

1. 中秋節是陽曆八月十五日。　　　　___對　___錯

2. 中秋節是中國人全家團圓的日子。　___對　___錯

3. 中秋節全家人一起吃春餅、賞月。　___對　___錯
bǐng shǎng

4. 月餅是圓的，代表團圓。　　　　　___對　___錯

九　朗讀課文三遍

第六課

一 寫生詞

不	料										
悲	哀										
撕	裂										
不	肯										
嬌	女										
至											
波	濤	洶	涌								
勿											
吾											
以	…	…	為	榮							
填	平										
依	然										

9

中國神話傳説

但	願										

投											

發	誓										

二　組詞

料＿＿＿＿　　哀＿＿＿＿　　撕＿＿＿＿　　肯＿＿＿＿

蒼＿＿＿＿　　濤＿＿＿＿　　填＿＿＿＿　　淹＿＿＿＿

奪＿＿＿＿　　誓＿＿＿＿　　嬌＿＿＿＿　　依＿＿＿＿

洶＿＿＿＿　　願＿＿＿＿　　投＿＿＿＿　　取＿＿＿＿

三　詞語解釋

1. 不料——

2. 不斷——

四　造句

1. 不料＿＿＿＿＿＿＿＿＿＿＿＿＿＿＿＿＿＿＿＿＿

2. 不肯＿＿＿＿＿＿＿＿＿＿＿＿＿＿＿＿＿＿＿＿＿

3. 決心＿＿＿＿＿＿＿＿＿＿＿＿＿＿＿＿＿＿＿＿＿

五 根據課文判斷對錯

1. 炎帝有一位愛女，名叫女娃。 ＿＿對 ＿＿錯

2. 女娃去東海邊遊玩淹死了。 ＿＿對 ＿＿錯

3. 女娃變成一只美麗的小雞。 ＿＿對 ＿＿錯

4. 炎帝打獵時，一只燕子在他的頭上飛。 ＿＿對 ＿＿錯

5. 精衛鳥決心填平大海。 ＿＿對 ＿＿錯

六 根據課文填空

1. 精衛鳥的聲聲哀叫，天地也被＿＿＿＿＿＿了。

2. 山林還是那樣蒼翠啊，我女兒卻＿＿＿＿＿＿在海中！

3. ＿＿＿＿＿＿再也無法說話了，父親是多麼的＿＿＿＿＿＿！

4. 大海為什麼不能被＿＿＿＿＿＿呢！波浪依然洶涌！

七 朗讀課文三遍

11

中國神話傳說

第八課

一 寫生詞

倉												
繩												
牲	口											
一	圈											
賬	目											
減	少											
記	憶											
蹄	印											
創	造											
合	適											
排	列											
格	子											
乘												

第八課

防											
串	連										

二　組詞

示＿＿＿＿　　　繩＿＿＿＿　　　牲＿＿＿＿　　　圈＿＿＿＿

賬＿＿＿＿　　　增＿＿＿＿　　　減＿＿＿＿　　　煩＿＿＿＿

蹄＿＿＿＿　　　獸＿＿＿＿　　　笨＿＿＿＿　　　創＿＿＿＿

格＿＿＿＿　　　適＿＿＿＿　　　列＿＿＿＿　　　憶＿＿＿＿

三　選字組詞

| 記　口　目　獸　麻　加　減　笨　印　造 |

牲＿＿＿＿　　　賬＿＿＿＿　　　增＿＿＿＿　　　＿＿＿＿少

＿＿＿＿煩　　　蹄＿＿＿＿　　　鳥＿＿＿＿　　　創＿＿＿＿

＿＿＿＿憶　　　＿＿＿＿重

四　寫出反義詞

增加——　　　　　笨重——　　　　　麻煩——

13

五 詞語解釋

1. 牲口——

2. 明顯——

3. 表示——

六 造句

1. 增加＿＿＿＿＿＿＿＿＿＿＿＿＿＿＿＿＿＿

2. 減少＿＿＿＿＿＿＿＿＿＿＿＿＿＿＿＿＿＿

3. 整齊＿＿＿＿＿＿＿＿＿＿＿＿＿＿＿＿＿＿

4. 合適＿＿＿＿＿＿＿＿＿＿＿＿＿＿＿＿＿＿

七 根據課文判斷對錯

1. 遠古時期,沒有文字。人們是用結繩

   記事的。　　　　　　　＿＿對　＿＿錯

2. 相傳倉頡是黃帝手下的官。　＿＿對　＿＿錯

3. 相傳倉頡看見雪地上動物的蹄印,創

   造了最早的象形文字。　　　＿＿對　＿＿錯

八 寫一寫傳説人物《造字神——倉頡》（最少寫八句話）

_____

_____

_____

_____

_____

_____

_____

九 朗讀課文三遍

第二課聽寫

第四課聽寫

第六課聽寫